Contagious Joy

Contagious Joy

❧

Joyful Devotions to Lift Your Spirits

Patsy Clairmont

Mary Graham

Barbara Johnson

Nicole Johnson

Marilyn Meberg

Luci Swindoll

Sheila Walsh

Thelma Wells

Mary Hollingsworth, *General Editor*

W PUBLISHING GROUP
A Division of Thomas Nelson Publishers
Since 1798

www.wpublishinggroup.com

W Publishing Group books may be purchased in bulk for educational, business, fundraising, or sales promotional use. For information, please e-mail SpecialMarkets@ThomasNelson.com.

Scripture references are from the following sources:

The Holy Bible, New International Version (NIV). Copyright © 1973, 1978, 1984. International Bible Society. Used by permission of Zondervan Bible Publishers. The New King James Version (NKJV), copyright © 1979, 1980, 1982, Thomas Nelson, Inc., Publishers. The Message (MSG), copyright © 1993. Used by permission of NavPress Publishing Group. The King James Version of the Bible (KJV). The Holy Bible, New Century Version (NCV), copyright © 1987, 1988, 1991 by Word Publishing, a division of Thomas Nelson, Inc. Used by permission. Quotations designated ASB are from the American Standard Bible, © 1901. Quotations designated NASB are from the New American Standard Bible, © 1960, 1977 by the Lockman Foundation. Quotations designated TLB are from the *Living Bible* copyright © 1971 by Tyndale House Publishers, Wheaton, Ill. Used by permission.

Herman Hesse, "Happiness [603]", *Reflections*, (New York: Farrar, Straus and Giroux, 1974), 167.

Editorial Staff: Shady Oaks Studio, Bedford, Texas
Cover Design: Studio Olika, Cincinnati, Ohio

Library of Congress Cataloging-in-Publication Data

Contagious joy! : joyful devotions to lift your spirits / Patsy Clairmont . . . [et al.]; Mary Hollingsworth, general editor.
   p. cm.
   Summary: "Devotional written by Women of Faith authors to help bring joy into everyday living"—Provided by publisher.

ISBN 0-8499-0048-4 (hardcover)
ISBN 10: 0-8499-0048-4
ISBN 13: 978-0-8499-0048-8

1. Christian women—Religious life. 2. Joy—Religious aspects—Christianity. I. Clairmont, Patsy.   II. Hollingsworth, Mary, 1947–
BV4527.C655   2006
242'.643—dc22   2005030212

Printed in the United States of America
06 07 08 09 10 QWP 9 8 7

Contents

꙳ ✳ ꙳

Introduction
Contagious Joy
  Mary Hollingsworth ix

Part I Joy Welcomes
Putting Out the Welcome Mat
  Mary Graham 3

Y'all Come!
  Patsy Clairmont 9

Behind-the-Scenes Welcome
  Thelma Wells 15

God in Full View!
  Marilyn Meberg 21

Living in God's House
  Luci Swindoll 27

Part 2 Joy Embraces
My Friend, Joy
  Nicole Johnson 35

Celestial Moments
  Luci Swindoll 41

Embracing the Book
  Patsy Clairmont 47

God's Gift Bearers
  Sheila Walsh 52

There's Nothing Like a
Mother's Embrace . . .
Except the Father's
  Barbara Johnson 57

Part 3 Joy Whispers
If You'll Talk, He'll Listen
  Thelma Wells 65

Pitcher This
  Patsy Clairmont 71

Latitude of Longing
  Nicole Johnson 77

Unspeakable Joy
  Mary Graham 83

Too Happy to Hold Back
  Barbara Johnson 89

Part 4 Joy Celebrates
Celebration!
  Patsy Clairmont 97

Filling Your Blessing Basket
  Sheila Walsh 103

Not Too Tick and Not Too
Tin
  Marilyn Meberg 109

God Is in Control
  Mary Graham 115

Celebrating Wonder
  Nicole Johnson 121

Part 5 Joy Laughs
Tea Time and Supper
  Marilyn Meberg 129

Look for the Laugh
  Barbara Johnson 134

An Attitude of Gratitude
Produces Praise, Joy, and
Laughter
  Thelma Wells 140

Laughing Later
  Nicole Johnson 146

The Moustache-Waxing
Moments of Life
  Sheila Walsh 153

Part 6 Joy Sings
Joy from the Ruins
  Sheila Walsh 161

A Greenroom Hallelujah!
  Marilyn Meberg 167

Love Fills Your Heart with
Joy
  Thelma Wells 173

Hit Parade
  Patsy Clairmont 179

Singing My Heart Out to God
  Luci Swindoll 185

Part 7 Joy Encourages
Mansions and Bridges
  Luci Swindoll 193

Mama T's Love for Mentoring
  Thelma Wells 199

A Christmas to Remember
  Mary Graham 206

Come On, You Can Do It
  Barbara Johnson 212

Flying with a Limp
  Marilyn Meberg 218

Part 8 Joy Applauds
Exuberant with Applause
  Barbara Johnson 225

Reading Between the Lines
  Luci Swindoll 231

Say It Loud and Clear!
  Sheila Walsh 237

Remembering Grace
  Mary Graham 243

A Standing Ovation for God
  Nicole Johnson 249

Conclusion:
Her Name Was Joy
  Mary Hollingsworth . . . 255

About the Authors 257

Contagious Joy

MARY HOLLINGSWORTH

✿

*H*ow long has it been since you played Giggle Belly? If you're like me, probably quite a while (how about fifty years?). But don't you remember when you were a kid at a slumber party, and someone would say, "Hey, I know! Let's play Giggle Belly!" Everyone would instantly agree, because it was so much fun.

The first girl laid down on the floor on her back with her head on a pillow. The second girl put her head on the stomach of the first one, and the third one put her head on the stomach of the second one. And on it went until everyone was stretched out across the room with their heads on one another's stomachs.

The first girl would say "Ha!" with as much "H" as possible to make her stomach bounce, which in turn bounced the head of the second girl. Then the second one said, "Ha! Ha!" The third one said, "Ha! Ha! Ha!" And each time they did, their stomach bounced, making the head of the next girl bounce too. By the time you got to number four, who said, "Ha! Ha! Ha! Ha!" the whole room had exploded into uproarious laughter, because the laughter had been passed down the line to the last girl at the very end. What fun!

Joy is like that too—it gets passed along to others. It's contagious! Infectious. It causes outbreaks of hope and delirious laughter, resulting in unexplainable peace.

Joy is caught from those who already have it, and then you inadvertently expose others to it, whether you really intend to or not, like the measles. It spreads like a West Texas wildfire! And it can't be stopped easily. Injecting the infected person with life's troubles won't eliminate joy. Swallowing sorrows and pain won't eradicate it. Even large doses of grief only hide its symptoms temporarily. Soon joy breaks out again, like the seven-year itch. It just won't go away.

People who are infected with joy show several obvious symptoms that help you diagnose them immediately as carriers of joy. If you go to their home to visit them, they'll throw open the door and welcome you with a warm embrace, just as if nothing's wrong. But be careful! Remember, joy is highly contagious. You might catch it!

You'll also know joyful people by the way they laugh and sing and celebrate life all the time. (You'd think they *like* being joyful or something!) You can see them whispering words of joy to people who are sad or lonely, and when someone finally does catch joy from them, they applaud like crazy. Now I ask you, is that a Christian way to act?

Another game we played as kids where we passed things on to others was Gossip. Everyone sat in a circle. The first girl whispered something in the ear of the second girl. Maybe it was something like, "Silly Sally sold seashells by the seashore." Then the second girl whispered it in the ear of the third girl, and on it went around the circle. When it got to the last girl in the circle, she had to say aloud what she had heard. And it usually came out nothing like what the first girl had said: "I saw Sally stealing shoes at the shoe store." Yikes!

I hear that joy is *not* like that. It doesn't become weaker or distorted when it's passed along. It just gets better, like my leftover Yum Yum Cake that becomes more moist and delicious the longer it sits. (Of course, you may be wondering, *If it's so wonderful, why is there any left over?* Does your mama know you ask such rude questions?)

Evidently there are several effective ways to avoid catching joy. According to the people I talked to, just use any of these, and you won't catch it:

- *Avoid getting close to God.* He's the most contagious Joygiver of all. If you stay away from him, you're guaranteed not to catch his joy. For instance, one of his followers said, "Being with you, God, will fill me with joy" (Psalm 16:11 NCV).

- *Don't read his Book*. Consistent exposure to his teachings on joy will infiltrate your mind and heart. Just put it on a shelf and forget it. One of his people said this: "Your statutes are my heritage forever; they are the joy of my heart" (Psalm 119:111 NIV).

- *Isolate yourself from joyful people*. You simply can't be around these happy, laughing, hospitable folks and escape becoming joyful yourself. It's inevitable. His Book says, "The followers were filled with joy" (Acts 13:52 NCV).

- *Don't pray!* Prayer puts you in direct contact with God and brings certain exposure to joy. Here's what his own Son said: "Ask and you will receive, so that your joy will be the fullest possible joy" (John 16:24 NCV).

- *And whatever you do, don't use this devotional book!* The authors of these messages are hopelessly eaten up with joy. It has overrun their minds and hearts to the point that they are giddy with hope. They've sold out to God completely. (And I hear they're trying to infect us all!)

That's it, friends. I've given you fair warning. Read this book at your own risk. And remember that once you've caught joy, you will never recover.

༄

No one can take away your joy.
John 16:22 NIV

PART I

❧

Joy Welcomes

Putting Out the Welcome Mat

MARY GRAHAM

ᨃ ✳ ᨃ

Be hospitable to one another without grumbling.
(1 PETER 4:9 NKJV)

*W*hen I was a child growing up in a large family and a small home, we always had company. The picture is still fresh in my mind.

My parents had families who either lived nearby or came to our house for vacations, holidays, and weekends. We lived in a small, neighborly community in Oklahoma, and my mother had a close circle of lifelong friends who often came to visit over a cup of coffee or a glass of iced tea.

Most summer evenings, ten, twenty, or more neighbors and relatives ended up at our house on the front porch. When they did, there was talking, laughing, storytelling (*mostly* storytelling), and joy. Immoderate joy, really, that welcomed everyone to come in and make themselves at home. And it happened all the time. Even when the Avon lady came, she stayed all day. Pity her other customers.

It didn't seem odd to me at the time that no one ever invited us to their homes. I now know we were way too many to entertain. Having us to your home would be like inviting a small country to dinner.

When my sisters and brothers grew up, they imitated my parents. Their doors were always open and welcoming to friends and strangers. They had larger homes and nicer places to practice hospitality, but their hearts were like my parents', and they imitated what they'd learned. Those homes were places of shared joy and a most welcoming place to be.

When I was in college, I had the habit of bringing people home with me. It didn't matter if I was going to my parents' home or one of my sisters', I brought people along. There was never a question about whether or not someone would be in my tow when I came home. The question was how many and how long would we stay.

Having spent all of my adult life in ministry, that hospitality trend has continued. Because of my parents, it's always seemed natural to bring people home with me. I've brought them home when they needed someplace to stay, or when they were sick, or hurting, or hungry, or for no other reason than that I enjoyed the pleasure of their company.

In 2005, one by one, and through a variety of circumstances, the core speaker team of Women of Faith transplanted themselves near Dallas. Thelma Wells already lived here, Nicole

Johnson has had a semipermanent residence in a Dallas suburb for a couple of years, and after ten years of traveling together, Luci Swindoll, Sheila Walsh, Marilyn Meberg, and Patsy Clairmont bought houses here and moved in lock, stock, and barrel (maybe just to keep from having to change planes every weekend in Dallas).

Since our little community has been established, I've noticed this team is an extremely hospitable bunch. For example, last night we were invited to Luci's for dinner. She had a houseguest, and the two of them shopped and cooked all day in preparation. Luci set a gorgeous table so that the rest of us did little but ooh and aah all night. After dinner we played a fun, verbal, interactive game, hooting, hollering, and laughing our heads off. We felt refreshed and nourished, not just because we'd eaten a scrumptious homemade dinner, but we'd fed our souls in the sweet and satisfying fellowship of the evening.

And that's when it hit me: hospitality is underrated! It's not just an old-fashioned idea that people used to have time to enjoy because life was duller and less complicated. Hospitality is God's idea. It's a joyful, welcoming idea.

First Peter 4:9 says, "Be hospitable to one another without grumbling" (NKJV). That's in the context of the verse before that which says to love one another fervently, and the following verse, which says minister to each other. Practicing hospitality is important to God and us. Jesus loved to be with his friends and followers, and we often find him in their homes.

As I look back through the years, I'm encouraged by the relationships that have been built simply through opening my home. In the 1980s, I worked in a ministry with a team of people who, for the most part, were couples with small children. One year I had a party on Easter after church for those families. For almost ten years after that, I did it every Easter. We had as many as seventy people, playing games appropriate for people of all ages, hunting eggs, doing talent shows, telling stories, eating, playing, laughing, and singing. The parties lasted from noon to night.

Those events became huge affairs, and every year I wondered if we could keep doing them. They were time-consuming to plan, a bit expensive to host, and quite challenging to entertain as many as fifty children of all ages. The parties were just too enjoyable not to have, and they became a highlight of our year. It wasn't unusual for people to call and ask if a friend of a friend could please get on the invitation list or if they could bring out-of-town relatives. And why? Because we had so much fun.

Finally the crowds outgrew my home. The mission organization of which I was a member started doing the parties on the lawn of our headquarters and sold tickets to anyone who wanted to come. Maybe they still do.

As wonderful as those events were, it's the sweet memory that has outlasted everything else and become the best part. The sweetest thing of all is that now those children are grown. Many of them are in full-time ministry, and I hear from them regularly. I keep up with them and now *their* children. From time to time they mention how much they loved those parties and even how they've established similar traditions.

I realize those parties were one of the main reasons I ever had a relationship with those (then) little boys and girls. I would have known their parents, but I wouldn't have known them if I hadn't done what they could enjoy. Getting on their level enabled me to open a little door into their worlds and step gently inside. Even though I was (and am still) single and childless, practicing hospitality was the key to knowing many children personally who have now grown up to be leaders in their generation. That's one of the rewards of hospitality.

I had a very dear friend who, through a very traumatic event in her life several years ago, quite suddenly remembered having suffered serious sexual abuse as a child. She went almost overnight from being a strong, mature, capable leader in her world to being like a small, frightened, insecure, almost inept little girl. I had no idea what to do. She was getting professional help, but she really couldn't function day to day. I was at a loss to help. So I did what my mother would do—I took her home with me. She was there a few weeks and, trust me, it was hard on everyone. Finally, she was admitted to a psychiatric hospital where she began a slow, painful healing. For a few years, during the darkest days, she stayed with me.

Today, my friend is a renowned Christian therapist and one of the leading experts on sexual abuse in the country. She has a unique niche in ministry—although a victim, she does her best work with those who victimize others. She works with abusers and perpetrators, because she understands that people don't become predators in a vacuum but through some horrific circumstances of their own. Frankly, I'm amazed at her genius and giftedness. It's my great reward that God put it on my heart to practice hospitality at a time she needed it most.

My friend and four other women from that era in my life twenty years ago are now spread from Portland to Paris. We still gather at my house once a year for an intensive weekend of catching up and praying for one another. We have so much history that the weekends are spent just talking. Having invested so much in one another's lives all these years, we understand the value of being together even though now we can only manage it annually. "Same time next year" has taken on new meaning for us.

I have many friends and family members who have, at a point in time, all but wrapped me in a blanket of love and taken me home with them when I've needed it most. They've put me to bed, brought me meals, prayed for me, and nursed me back to health and strength either physically, emotionally, or spiritually. They've been the Good Samaritans in my life, and it has been my joy to be welcomed by them when I've needed it most.

Hospitality is not the idea of a few random folks. It's God's idea—and a great one at that. It is kingdom work. Be welcoming. There's no greater joy.

~ *And Lord, we know that you welcome us into your home when this life is over. We anticipate with joy the day that we sit down to the heavenly meal we will share in your presence. And we pray that we'll bring a few friends along with us when we come. In Jesus's name, amen.*

Y'all Come!

Patsy Clairmont

ᔓ ✳ ᔓ

I was a stranger and you took Me in. (Matthew 25:25 NKJV)

One of the qualities of the state of Texas that I love the most is the way its people wholeheartedly welcome others. From my first visit in the early 1980s I was smitten with the widespread congeniality and open-door hospitality. Yet even having established that endearing reputation with me years ago, I never planned to live there. Then it happened. Thelma Wells's daughter Vickie was getting married, and I didn't want to miss the celebration. So I flew down to Dallas for three days to attend the festivities, and when I returned to Michigan I was a Texas homeowner. Yeehaw!

It started out innocently when my husband, Les, called me on my way to the wedding and asked me to look at houses in Texas to see what could be purchased for different prices. Notice he didn't say "buy one," nor did I have any plans of doing so; it was strictly a field trip. But when I stepped into the fourth house on my tour I was instantly smitten. I wasn't two feet into the house before it welcomed me as if I were a prodigal who'd finally found her way back. Every room sang, "You're home, you're home, welcome home!" Well, actually they sang, "Sweet Pea, y'all are home." Trust me, I heard that beckoning way down into my southern (Kentucky) roots.

Within weeks the transaction was made, and I was on a plane headed for the Lone Star State, the home of big, which is rather ironic when you consider my brief stature. Mary Graham, president of Women of Faith, and Ney Bailey, with whom Mary shares her house, invited me to stay with them while I was getting my home settled. The warmth of their embrace and the kindness of their inclusion was a balm to my did-I-make-the-right-decision soul. They reminded me of the verse in Matthew 25:35 that says, "I was a stranger, and you took me in."

For the first week, as I ran around shopping for everything from dust mops, dust pans, to dust ruffles (there's a lot of dust in Texas), I kept asking myself, *Patsy, what have you done?* But then Ney and Mary would reassure me that I had made a good decision (bless their hearts). In the evenings when I had even more time to second-guess myself (I get on my own last nerve), they filled our hours with visits, good food, and heart-happy laughter. What is there about shared laughter that knits hearts together while it unties mental tensions? Mary and Ney certainly made me feel drawn-in to my new surroundings and more settled even before I officially moved into my sweet dwelling.

Mary and Ney do not surprise me with their many kindnesses. I have known them long enough to observe their gift of welcoming people from all over the globe. It's not unusual to find folks from the four corners of the world "hiding out" in their home. In fact, I've been taking notes on how they do so much for so many and still maintain their own callings. First, may I say it is not easy to welcome the world into our worlds, because we are all so busy. I get exhausted just thinking of it, and I love people. But Ney and Mary have figured out how to do it with style and grace while bebopping through their own demanding pace.

Here's what I noted from my observations that would help us say with vigor, "Y'all come."

Flexibility. To be welcoming, one must have relaxed structure. To have no schedule is to invite chaos to enter in and set up housekeeping. We all need strategies in place as well as daily goals. Yet in our plans we need to make room for God's plans, which may, like a guest, arrive unexpectedly . . . with baggage. Flexibility is a prime factor for open arms.

Warmth. This isn't something you can have installed, like a furnace—it's generated from the heart. Both Mary and Ney exude acceptance and genuine caring toward the lives of others, which creates an environment for sweet fellowship. I'm not surprised that folks line up at their door in hopes of being lavished with personalized attention. Who doesn't long to feel received and heard?

Provision. Making preparations for guests translates into comfort and relaxation for all involved. There's nothing worse than to be in someone's home and sense that they were not prepared for your arrival, and, therefore, it's an inconvenience for you to be there.

Mary always made certain the guest bedroom and bath had all the necessary accoutrements . . . and then some (even a too-die-for cozy housecoat hung behind the bathroom door). She and Ney have a way of thinking of things they can do that are so specific to their guests' needs. For instance, Mary had a classy key ring for me, not only for my new house key to go on, but it had their house key attached so I felt free to come and go as I needed. They had a personalized greeting written to me on their chalkboard when I arrived, making me feel planned for and welcomed. And in the mornings Ney drew maps, so that on my way to Kroger I didn't end up in Honduras. She laid out my breakfast needs so I could quickly be out the door and off to my house business.

Schedule. Give guests a general schedule for each day. Mary and Ney kept me informed of their agenda so I could plan accordingly. If they had to leave before I got up, they would leave a message for me on the counter. It was a thoughtful gesture that helped me step through my day without fear of messing up theirs. And they made sure I had their cell phone numbers so I could reach them.

Time. Even though Mary and Ney maintained full work schedules while I was there, they always took time to be with me. I never had the sense when we sat down to visit that they were mentally somewhere else. Being fully engaged in your guest's conversation communicates your welcome more than anything else you do. They didn't toe-tap, finger-thump, or sit on the edges of their chairs, but in a relaxed comfortable way they showed interest by focusing and asking questions.

Welcoming others out of this wind-whipped world into the sanctuary of our homes is a true ministry. Sometimes those who cross our thresholds are in dire need of safety, safe ears to hear their hearts, safe words to direct their paths, or just the safety that acceptance offers. Yet some folks are not assured of how others may receive them . . . remember the prodigal?

That New Testament young man went through a disintegration of character when he demanded his inheritance while his father was still living, and then he squandered his money until he was left penniless and humiliated. Reduced to eating food from a pig's trough, the runaway finally came to his senses. That's when his thoughts turned toward home and all it now represented to him. He wanted to return, but he knew he didn't deserve his father's mercy, so he was prepared to be a servant to his dad, if he would only take him back.

Dad saw his prodigal son in the distance and stopped what he was doing (flexibility) and rushed to meet his son and fell on his neck and kissed him (warmth). Then the father sent a servant to bring out a robe, a ring, and sandals for his wayward boy (provision) and arranged (schedule) to throw a party (time) to celebrate his return.

Imagine how the prodigal must have felt dragging his sorry

self home only to have the reception of his life. That unconditional love and acceptance must have taken his breath away. I'm sure he was deeply grateful and properly humbled

Actually, I don't have to imagine, because I was a prodigal; but in my story my mom was the father from the Bible account. As a rebellious and troubled teenager I ran away, which caused great heartache for my family. When I returned broke and ashamed that I had pulled such a stunt, my mom ran out of the house with open arms, embraced me, and covered me with her tears. I will never forget that moment. (I just knew Mom would throttle me and that I'd never hear the end of the trouble I caused. The truth is, my New Testament mom never spoke of it again.)

The prodigal's redemptive story is a touching picture of God's welcome-home heart toward us. Imagine, he's not waiting, arms tightly crossed with a righteous scowl on his face to remind us of our wayward behavior. Rather he waits with open arms to lavish us with his unconditional love so that we might experience welcome-home joy!

᠅   *Dear Father, it is so wonderful to be your child—your often wayward child—and to know that I can always come home to you. I run into your warm embrace and listen hard for the words I long to hear you say: "Welcome home, my child. Welcome home." Amen.*

Behind-the-Scenes Welcome
THELMA WELLS
꙳ ✹ ꙳

My Presence will go with you, and I will give you rest.
(EXODUS 33:14 NIV)

*A*s a banking manager year ago, I supervised thirty-seven women at one time. Do you think we were on the road to contagious joy? I don't think so! At first, each of them was going down a different highway trying to get to the same place.

One woman was a tattletale and watched what everyone else was doing so she could come tell me. I had to set her on Highway Straight. So I assigned her the *responsibility* of watching everybody to see if they were working, taking personal phone calls, clocking in late or leaving early. Her instructions were to document all this, and when she got enough information on one of her coworkers, to bring her with her documentation to my office so we could handle the situation expeditiously. This assignment was just a bit too open-ended for her, so she straightened out quickly.

15

Another employee just *had* to leave early several days a week to either get a body wrap, nails done, pedicure, facial hair removed, or go to the weight center. She was on Beautification Lane. After a few months on that unjoyful journey, I had to put her on Highway Termination so she could do all those things unencumbered.

Arriving at work late was the journey of another employee. Sure, she had small children and had little help at home. This took some strategizing. But working with the personnel office, I found Highway Flexibility for her. We made it possible for her to clock in later in the mornings and remain later in the evenings.

This and so much more went on behind the scenes of the banking job, but the end result was that people were rerouted to Highway Teamwork and joy was restored. In fact, people enjoyed their jobs so much that my turnover halted, and stability was the order of the day. We were back on a joyful journey.

If you know the story of Moses's journey in the wilderness with those two million people he supervised, as you look behind the scenes, you must know that his burden was enormous. Just imagine all those folks waiting in line to talk to you about their problems and grumbling all the time.

Just like at the bank, a woman had to put her two cents' worth in and start the teamwork process. Zipporah told her daddy, Jethro, about her husband being stressed to the max and asked him to come up with a solution. (The Bible doesn't say this, but I know women because I *am* one. We are take-charge people, but we let the men think they've done it all by themselves.) Moses welcomed delegation instructions from his father-in-law and created a system of teamwork that has been passed down from generation to generation. You go, Moses! Moses's wilderness journey became a lot more enjoyable when he organized qualified people into teams and gave them responsibility and accountability to him as their manager. Everybody got in on the joy of helping others do the work needed for them to survive their journey along Wilderness Way to the Promised Land.

There's a certain curiosity about how things tick. We want to know what's going on behind the scenes, don't we? I can just imagine that some of you want to know the workings behind the scenes of the Women of Faith conferences. I did. It's fascinating!

So much goes on behind the scenes to make each Women of Faith conference excellent—a place that welcomes you warmly when you come. In fact, I believe it is the best-run professional organization of its kind and size in the world. And it takes the entire team to pull one together.

Team is an acronym that means **T**ogether **E**veryone **A**ccomplishes **M**ore. This team consists of competent and enthusiastic directors who make the major decisions for Women of Faith with our president, Mary Graham. It's so funny: people see Mary Graham announcing the programs in the arena and think, *Anybody can do what she's doing.* That's not true, of course, even though it may look easy to some. Mary brings to the table wit, charm, decisiveness, quality control, audience control, hospitality, gentleness but firmness, and some of the most successful leadership skills of anyone in the land. She works tirelessly and with integrity, side by side with several high-ranking executives in our home office.

Announcing the program is a holiday in the park compared to what she does every day—managing her directors; working with the officers of our parent company, Thomas Nelson, Inc.; and doing her best to corral the speaker team called Porch Pals. Her burden is heavy! But check this out: she's a woman and can multitask brilliantly.

Back at the office in Plano, Texas, is the capable staff, whose vital roles are to take your telephone calls, give you information, or take your reservations. If you've ever called for reservations, you know what kind of warm welcome and quality customer service you receive. That's not by accident; that's on purpose. You're the most valuable asset Women of Faith has.

Scott and Ed add their leadership brilliance to the lighting and technical staff, who create the scenery and ambiance in every arena. Every venue is transformed into a sanctuary of praise and worship by these folks. It's a production of skills and abilities that exceed any others I've seen. When you attend a conference, notice the changing lighting, the configuration of the stage, the comfortable chairs the speakers sit in, and the television monitors throughout the arena. That stuff doesn't just appear. It has to be set up, checked, adjusted all day long, and put back up at night with such precision. When it's loaded on the trucks, it has to be categorized and organized so it's in place to set up quickly at the next conference. Within thirty minutes after the conference ends, the arena is cleared out and the trucks are loaded.

Parked at each site are the shiny eighteen-wheelers that are driven by our excellent transportation engineers, who ensure that the equipment arrives at the next venue on time. These are the sweetest men. They're gentle and kind, polite and courteous. It's a genuine pleasure to associate with them.

Suppose you want to come to the conference and you speak Spanish as your first language. Not to fret—we've got Spanish interpreters ready to welcome you and help you understand every word spoken at the conference. Or perhaps you need sign-language interpretation. We've got that too!

It's beautiful to see people who are physically challenged find a comfortable and convenient place from which to enjoy the conference.

You may also get a chance to meet the bookstore and product-development people as they handle the challenges of the masses at the book tables. Their jobs are nonstop as they ship, receive, set up, and tear down the exhibit areas. My sincerest thanks to all those behind-the-scenes people for their commitment and dedication to Women of Faith.

There's another group that I never want to take for granted. It's the companions who travel with the speakers and guests from week to week, making sure we make our flights, find the hotels, and get to and from the conferences in one piece. This is not an easy job. Most of these precious people have traveled with us for nearly ten years. Thank you, companions!

Women of Faith is constantly working to make the conferences as easy as possible for you, the association member, and others who attend. We want to make sure when you arrive at a conference to "rest" for a weekend, you can truly find the respite you need for your soul. You, too, are part of our *team*. Your participation with us says, "We ain't tired yet either." We love you and appreciate you!

When the journey of working harmoniously behind the scenes is effective, that's teamwork. In it, there is an atmosphere of joy. Even Jesus told his disciples when he sent them out on their missionary journey that the worker was worthy of support (see Matthew 10:10).

Behind-the-scenes teamwork is essential, and teamwork requires everyone's contribution. When you get tired of trying to route people onto Highway Straight, just remember that God Almighty is always working behind the scenes on every highway we travel in life. Think about how he created a workable team for Moses, and chill out. God told Moses what he says to us every day, "My Presence will go with you, and I will give you rest" (Exodus 33:14 NIV). Welcome home.

Master of our highway journeys, what a joy to know that your presence leads us on every path we trod. It's comforting to know that you are working behind the scenes to help us move in the right direction until, at long last, we are welcomed into your presence for eternity. Amen.

God in Full View!

MARILYN MEBERG

ᨀ ✳ ᨀ

God-traveled, these roads curve up the mountain,
and at the last turn—Zion! God in full view! (PSALM 84:7 MSG)

*L*ast week I was visiting my daughter, Beth, and my two little grandsons, Alec and Ian. It was a perfect time to be there because I'm such a nut about trees. The spring leaves were vibrant with new green foliage, and since Beth's house sits under the protective custody of several huge elms, I thought I'd died and gone to heaven!

It was Tuesday morning. Beth and boys had gone to work and school leaving me in my accustomed spot under a tree. I was thumbing through *The Message* version of the Bible and landed on a portion of Psalm 84 that was entirely new to me. Where had I been? Where had it been? I had no idea, but it spoke to me. Scripture so frequently reminds us that we are never outside the realm of God's care or presence, but that message was especially

21

soft and inspiring as I read it that morning. It continues to be softly inspiring; I've read it every day since. I'd love to share some thoughts about it with you, but first let me refresh your memory of verses 5–7: "And how blessed all those in whom you live, whose lives become roads you travel; they wind through lonesome valleys, come upon brooks, discover cool springs and pools brimming with rain! God-traveled, these roads curve up the mountain, and at the last turn—Zion! God in full view!" (MSG).

What a beautifully loving image that my life is a road God travels. And the road (my life) has lonely valleys that include his presence, his full knowledge, and his consistent encouragement. I'm not in the valley on my own, counting the days until God comes back. God never left. During times of extreme pain we so often feel lonely and without a source of divine comfort. It's as if God is on "standby." We don't sense his presence and our circumstances scream out, "You're on your own, baby!" Not the truth. God is walking our life road, and that includes the valleys.

One of my more heartbreaking valleys has been to witness the tormented mind and life of my Aunt Florence, who first evidenced the beginning signs of schizophrenia at the age of twelve. Prior to that time, Florence had been a witty, fun-loving, gregarious little girl. Her gradual transformation was a mystery to my mother and my grandparents. She was twenty-five when a formal diagnosis of schizophrenia was made. Throughout the years of her interior anguish, she consistently remained gentle and kind. She was never violent and never a danger to those around her. I have always adored her.

As a child it gave me great pleasure to make her laugh. I wasn't sure then why this gentle soul sat slumped in a chair staring endlessly at the floor. But a light would come into her eyes when I began my "clowning." She'd always say, "My little Marilyn, you are so funny." I've never in my life received more gratifying praise than those softly spoken words.

When I was four years old, hoping to yet again draw Aunt Florence out of her reverie, I asked her if I could drive her car. She never refused me anything, so I wasn't surprised when she said, "Of course you can drive my car." I have absolutely no memory of where my parents were or where my grandmother was when this concession was made to me, but I had a vague sense it lacked wisdom.

I sat on her lap steering while she tended to the gas pedal. Though I was unfamiliar with Mr. Magoo at that time, I think a parallel could be drawn between his offhanded sightlessness and my tendency to head for obstacles. Aunt Florence had her thumb and forefinger on the bottom of the steering wheel enabling us to clear a tree and trash can in good time. She didn't seem concerned about the meandering pattern we made down the middle of the little street behind our house or my side trips to the curb. It was the greatest joyride of my life. As we walked back into the house, I thanked her profusely for letting me drive. She took my hand and merely said, "My little Marilyn."

Time passed and little Marilyn grew up. One of my adult concerns has always been the safety and well-being of my Aunt Florence. She preferred her reclusive lifestyle and living in her childhood home in Cortez, Colorado. When I begged her to come live with me in California, she quietly and consistently refused. I visited her as often as I could.

Our final time together was last year. She was by then a reluctant resident of Golden Years Retirement Home and receiving great care. At the age of ninety-one, and having had several strokes, I wasn't sure she would recognize me when I walked into the kitchen where she was eating lunch. I pulled up a stool next to her and said, "Hi, sweetheart, do you know who I am?" She drew back and stared a second. Then she said, "You're Marilyn, but what in the world has happened to you?" I explained to her that I had grown old. She found that hard to grasp, and most of the day she would steal glances that told me she was sorry about what had happened to me.

On February 8, 2005, Aunt Florence died. She was ninety-two. For the first time in her life, her road led to a place of peace. It "curve[d] up the mountain, and at the last turn—Zion! God in full view!" It gives me pleasure to imagine her joyful welcome. I can see God opening his arms, scooping her up and softly whispering in her ear, "My little Florence."

Though this life-conclusion for Aunt Florence comforts me beyond words, I have to confess I've struggled with the why of her anguish on this earth. Psalm 84 says after the "lonesome valleys" the travelers come "upon brooks, discover cool springs and pools brimming with rain" (v. 6 MSG). Aunt Florence never experienced brooks, cool springs, or pools brimming with rain here on earth. She knew only the valley.

Some of you may also have known only the valley. You, too, may wonder why the refreshments of life have seemingly been for others and not for you. What's the answer to the heart sigh, *Why Lord? Why the pain? What's the point?*

The reality is there is no answer for what appears to be random pain placed on some and not others. Of course, we know we live in a sin-dominated world. That sin came after the free-choice decision to disobey God was carried out by Adam and Eve. We know from that time of self-centered arrogance, we have been living with the consequence of their sin-choice.

Does that explanation satisfy our need to understand why some continue to live without the "cool springs"? Quite frankly, it doesn't satisfy me. I need to understand the origin of evil. I need to understand that we all live in the tension that exists between good and evil. I need to understand that I live on a battlefield and not a playground. But in a clearly defined battle, I can choose sides. I choose God's side. I choose his enablement for my battles. I choose not to fight alone.

Aunt Florence didn't really have a choice. When the encompassing bleak darkness of mental illness infiltrated her mind, she was captive to its presence. She couldn't choose the cool waters after the valley, because she never left the valley. So where do we go with these quandaries and concerns? What do we say to ourselves about what appears to be an enormous injustice?

It is at this point I choose to relax and then rest in God's sovereign design. I don't know why her life was as it was. Deuteronomy 29:29 says, in effect, "There are secrets the Lord your God has not revealed to us." I can fuss and fume about whether God is entitled to keep secrets from me, or I can redirect my thinking to what is *not* secret about him—his nature of love. With love he created the world and all its people. With love he provided salvation for all who choose it. With love he walks our lives with us. Plain and simple. Reject it or accept it. God's love knows no boundaries and no one can "fathom what God has done from beginning to end" (Ecclesiastes 3:11 NIV). With a renewed quietness of heart, I choose to accept his sovereign love and sit with some unanswered questions.

In spite of Aunt Florence's schizophrenic mind, I know she knew Christ as her Savior. Her continual fear was that she was not good enough to be accepted by him. As of February 8, 2005, that fear and uncertainty is gone. I love to envision her face no longer etched in the reflected pain of her interior world but instead sitting under a huge, godly elm tree thinking, *I must have died and gone to heaven.*

Father, when our lives round the last curve in the road, let us know the incredible joy of seeing you in full view. We can't imagine what exhilaration that will be, but we yearn for that day to come quickly. Until that day, O Lord, hold us tightly in your arms. Amen.

Living in God's House
Luci Swindoll
ɔ❀ɔ

Practice hospitality. (ROMANS 12:13 NIV)

When I was little I had a set of Tinker Toys that I loved. Even now, I still love Tinker Toys. I've made bridges, houses, wagons, forts, cages, and furniture out of Tinker Toys.

And I love Lincoln Logs. By overlapping enough grooved ends, you can create the Roman Coliseum, albeit a kind of *rustic* version. But with enough imagination it has a resemblance. Sort of. And I love LEGOS. I've made everything from robots to rocket launchers with LEGOS. To this day, somebody gives me a little set of LEGOS every year for Christmas. I've missed my calling; I was meant to be a child. I love to make things.

That's why I jumped at the idea of building my own house. *It'll be made out of giant Lincoln Logs*, I thought. Not only that, there was something exciting about leaving California after thirty years and heading back to Texas, my childhood state. For the past six years, my friends here had welcomed me with open arms to stay in their guest room during the summer and fall (our busiest travel seasons at Women of Faith). Finally, in 2004, it made sense for me to actually relocate here; so now it was *my* opportunity to roll out a welcome mat.

After talking with a builder and choosing a lot in Frisco, north of Dallas and not far from the WOF office, the plans were put into place. The next thing I did was buy a "house book"—a big fat binder to keep all my drawings, doodlings, notes, and lists in one place. This undertaking was going to be, without doubt, one of the most interesting adventures I'd ever known—challenging, maddening, thrilling, exhilarating, and stupefying . . . sometimes on the same day or within the same hour, but I was up for it. After all, I was only seventy-two, and it sounded like child's play to actually *build* a dream house.

When I made the decision to leave California and head for Texas, I was inundated with offers from friends and even strangers to help.

Can I bring lunch? Can I help you pack? Can I drive with you to Texas? Can I feed your dog? Well, I didn't have a dog, but had I, somebody would have offered to feed him. When I got here, Texas was just as gracious in her welcome as California had been in her farewell. My Texas buddies and I watched my house go up in fits and spurts. We prayed over the foundation, walls, roof, and yard. We pooled our resources of time and money as some folks planned on-site picnics while others brought Starbucks and brownies.

The day it was time for my furniture to leave its storage place and waltz in the door, I had so many helpers they almost had to wear nametags. I even had matching black T-shirts made with a white logo reading, "Team Luci." My friends proved that now-famous Home Depot motto: "You can do it. We can help." They epitomized the Golden Rule of Scripture: "Do to others as you would have them do to you" (Luke 6:31 NIV). When everybody pitches in, the world seems like a better place and the work is a lot more fun, don't you think? Teamwork! A God-given concept.

I actually moved in on Labor Day. I signed all the papers thirty days before, but because of the warmth and love of the friends with whom I was staying, they encouraged me to take my time to settle in. "Keep the new house as your 'project,' Luci, but don't move in until you're ready." So I did exactly that. I loved that lingering spirit of acceptance and camaraderie.

Now that I'm *in here*, I'm having a great time. I have a 480-square-foot library with my collection of treasured books and paintings. I've unpacked boxes whose contents I hadn't seen in decades—love letters between my parents; my brothers' and my report cards from grammar, junior high, and high school; oil paintings by my mother and aunt; scrapbooks of my grandmothers'; old fishing gear of my dad's and granddad's. The list goes on. What fun to dig around in all that stuff.

I'm actually not settled yet, because I keep thinking of things to hang or move or alphabetize. Not long ago I put my old record collection in order. In every box, bag, corner, nook, and cranny there's something else to unwrap, unpack, undo, or unwind that's been tucked away for eons. It's a treasure trove from the past, the museum of my life. (Or maybe a packrat's hideout.)

My greatest joy is throwing parties, having meetings, doing photo shoots, and enjoying out-of-town friends in the guestroom. Marilyn Meberg gave me a plaque to hang at the front door that reads, "The ornament of a house is the friends who frequent it" (Ralph Waldo Emerson), and my house is always full of ornaments. And here's why: immediately after the foundation was poured, I came here (in the rain) with a few close friends and a screwdriver. Into the wet cement I carved an inscription that's become my precept: *This house is dedicated to God. 04/07/04. L. Swindoll.* Wringing wet that rainy night, all of us put our hands in the air and sang "To God Be the Glory." I don't know that I've ever been more excited or overwhelmed. I was building my first home, had just given it to God, planned to live here soon, and had committed myself to mortgage payments until I was 101. *Life doesn't get any better than that!*

Everything I do in this house is governed by that phrase, and I've said it to myself dozens of times since then: *This is God's house.* It first started when a group of us had a birthday bash here for my brother Chuck: *God's house!* And it continued when the Women of Faith executive staff held a meeting around my dining table: *God's house!* There have been six or eight video and photo shoots here where the library had to be completely rearranged and wires and microphones put in precarious places, but so what? It's *God's house.* When things go "bump" in the night or a strange noise occurs in my backyard, I go back to sleep with the assurance that I'm in good hands because this is *God's house*. I never forget it. The joy of that phrase welcomes me home and helps me reach out to others. Dedicating my home to him may be the best thing I ever did in my life. The onus of responsibility is off me, and the decisions for reaching out to others are already made. (Every now and then when I see a dust ball here or there, I do wonder why God never cleans his own house!)

I'm to the place where I keep the porch light on, the welcome mat out, and the Pizza Hut phone number in my billfold. You have no idea how far I've come from being a contented loner to the neighborhood Perle Mesta. I used to spend hours reading adventure books like *The Worst Journey in the World*, and now I'm designing new ideas for place cards for one of the best dinner parties on the planet. God not only enlarged my surroundings, but he enlarged my heart. It's a great feeling.

And I thought Tinker Toys, Lincoln Logs, and LEGOS were fun! This is much better. God has given me a dwelling place that carries with it a joy I've never known before, and it's his joy that flows over the edges and onto my guests. Patsy Clairmont wrote and had framed for me a lovely blessing that captures exactly what I experience here:

> May the doors of your home open with joy
>   and close with safety.
> May the views from your windows dance
>   with creation's beauty.

May the floors meander throughout your house,
spreading peace.
May your library serve up the wonders of the world.
May your studio reverberate with artistry.
May your fires spark wondrous conversations.
May the walls quickly fill with memories
to surround you with satisfaction.
May the rooftop never stop shouting "glory" to the heavens.
May you be warmed by God's love,
comforted by the hospitality of the Spirit,
and companioned by the ongoing presence of our Savior.

I'm honored to have that heartfelt blessing and the love and friendship of the one who wrote it.

The apostle Paul tells us in Romans 12:12–13, "Be glad for all God is planning for you. Be patient in trouble, and prayerful always. When God's children are in need, you be the one to help them out. And get into the habit of inviting guests home for dinner or, if they need lodging, for the night" (TLB).

The New International Version says, "Practice hospitality." That's not always easy with a busy lifestyle, but I figure if I keep practicing, one of the days I'll get the hang of it.

✧ *Father, I am so blessed to get to live in your house. I love its warmth and protection, its windows and doors that let your world and people in, its quiet peace and joyful respite. I promise to keep the welcome mat out, Father, especially for you. In Jesus's sweet name, amen.*

PART 2

❧

Joy Embraces

My Friend, Joy

NICOLE JOHNSON

∾ ✱ ∾

You will find your joy in the LORD. (ISAIAH 58:14 NIV)

$\mathcal{I}$ met her long before I knew her name; we actually go way back, Joy and I. As a little girl, she would be with me at times of pure delight: running through the sprinkler, holding a puppy, riding my bicycle, or playing ball in the yard after dark. But there were years that I didn't see much of Joy, and I mistakenly came to think that she only came to visit when I was happy. She appeared to me a fair-weather friend, and I found it hard to put much stock in her presence.

But finding faith in God and living through more of life's circumstances, Joy has proved to be a better friend than I had thought. I don't mean to imply that I know her completely, as I am still learning, but I definitely know her better than I did. I have come to respect Joy and welcome her presence in my life as often as she embraces me. Like a deep and complex friend, she has many layers and levels that have taken time to understand and appreciate.

Joy often arrives unannounced. She's not a planner and doesn't seem to decide until the last minute what she will do. She won't clear her calendar to fit into my life or schedule regular appointments with me. She shows up when she wants to, and she often leaves abruptly, and those aren't always my favorite qualities in a person. But Joy loves arriving as an unexpected surprise. Many have missed knowing Joy simply because they don't like surprises.

William Wordsworth was surprised by Joy. In one of his poems, he penned how the sudden surprise of Joy "impatient as the wind" made him quickly look around to share it with his love, and he's forlorn to discover that he had forgotten her death in that moment of Joy. C. S. Lewis was also *Surprised by Joy*. It is the title of his early autobiography that details how he came to faith in God. Additionally, a wonderful surprise later in his life was that Lewis fell in love and married a woman named Joy. He was literally and figuratively twice surprised by Joy.

Joy has surprised me by turning up, oddly, when things are going wrong. Tears may be streaming down my face, and then comes a little knock on my soul's door. She arrives bringing a great sense of peace and contentedness, like a little spring bouquet of flowers or a basket of warm bread.

I cannot manufacture the circumstances that bring Joy to me. She will not be controlled. She comes in response to something, always very spontaneous, like wonder or gratitude. Sometimes I don't know that she is there, until I look up and see her. It's then I wonder how long she had been there before I noticed. I've also discovered, if I try to count on her, or seek her out by herself, she is usually nowhere to be found.

Sometimes Joy is silent and even seems absent. But she is never mad or punishing as some people are when they're silent; she's just settled. She doesn't have to talk all the time or be loud to announce her presence. She's equally happy to sit and listen or throw a party. She doesn't need to be the center of attention; she is simply content to bring life to a party by helping in the celebration.

Joy embraces me in these ways, but also all kinds of people. She will hug a prostitute or wrap her arms around a hurting child. She is welcoming of anyone who needs a lift. She has been known to sit down with someone on a park bench and stay all through lunch, providing wonderful companionship and happiness. She is no respecter of persons, and no one knows or owns all of her. She is very generous to those who welcome her, and she withholds no good thing from those she frequently visits.

Joy is beautiful, but not physically. She is not unattractive in any way; it's just that her physical features are outshone by her essence. She glows, and in her brightness I've never been able to tell the color of her skin or eyes or the shape of her nose. I don't know her height, for sometimes she radiates glory from a high place, and other times she laughs and giggles like a small child, bidding me to play on the floor. She can be charming, constantly emanating innocence and warmth, but she is not a charmer. She is never haughty or vain, and Joy goes out of her way to be pleasant with everyone.

She has wonderful friends, and loves to introduce them, given the opportunity. I often find her with her friends because they hang out together and run around as a group. I've met them, and know their names by heart: Love, Peace, Kindness, Goodness, Faithfulness, Gentleness, and Self-Control. I have found that they all influence each other a great deal, as good friends do. The more time they spend together, the more they become like the other, and when I am with them, I am changed too.

But I have also seen Joy in company that doesn't seem to become her. I have walked into a hospital room with Suffering only to see Joy as well, sitting by the bed, holding a patient's hand. I wondered to myself, *What is she doing here? Does she really belong here?* But when I talk to the person I have come to see, she tells me that she, too, was surprised to find that Joy arrived along with Pain, but she was awfully glad she did. Her presence has a way of making all things better.

Many people get to know Joy better when they are going through a very difficult period in their lives. It comes as a shock when they discover, as I did, that she is not the fair-weather friend they first imagined or a bubbly, air-headed, emotional girl that distances herself from hardship. They see the family resemblance to her cousin Happiness, but they notice that she is altogether different, because Joy will stay in the midst of tough circumstances while Happiness tends to sneak away. Initially I thought it would hurt her reputation to be connected in any way to Suffering or Pain, but it doesn't seem to bother her in the least. She is Joy, and she simply continues being herself.

Joy is full of emotional intelligence, but she is simple. She doesn't have to understand how things work or what they mean in order to enjoy them. She is not incapable of understanding, but she loves taking things at face value. Her kindness and spirit of fun make her great company. She laughs a lot, and I mean a lot, but I have never seen her make fun of anyone else. Her humor comes freely and never at the expense of another. She is full of energy and verve, yet she is not manic or anxious. Sometimes she will gently tug on my sleeve when she wants to show me something, but she also knows how to put two fingers in her mouth and whistle as loud as a train if she needs to.

Joy is not wealthy, but neither is she poor. She is far too smart to be trapped by money, and she's content with what she has. For years, I've heard people talk about Joy as if she is cliquish with those who have a lot possessions or a great deal of money, but she has revealed that to be false time and again. I have seen her accompany a rich man on a family outing as well as a poor, homeless woman on the city streets. Joy is no respecter of money . . . or persons, for that matter. She regularly visits those in prison and will even visit those in prisons of their own making, as often as she is allowed entrance. Joy stands for freedom, but she knows it is found in the heart, not in the circumstances.

It would be impossible to describe her as thin or fat. Joy is healthy and robust and takes good care of herself. She treats her soul with kindness, and everyone else's as well. She loves to be in the company of those who are having a good time around the table, but it seems less about the food and more about those who have gathered to dine. She is almost always seated next to Gratitude, because they are very close. Joy will usually choose the chair farthest away from Selfishness. She has whispered to me that she finds the conversation lacking.

Joy comes to us from God. She is a gift to our lives and our hearts. He gives Joy to us that we might welcome her as we would a good friend whom we trust. He wants us to get to know Joy so that our relationship with her is full and complete, and so that Joy will be our strength.

৵ *Thank you, God, for giving us Joy. May she regularly visit our hearts and homes, embracing us with her joyful presence and reminding us of you. Amen.*

Celestial Moments

LUCI SWINDOLL

_ゃ_ ❊ _ゃ_

Respond to the greatness of our God!
(DEUTERONOMY 32:3 MSG)

$\mathcal{T}$he request that came to me through the Women of Faith office from a woman in northern California was very unusual. Someone was asking if it would be possible for her friend, Anne, to meet and have lunch with me sometime soon. Occasionally, I get those kinds of requests, although they're pretty rare.

This case was different from all the others, though. Anne is dying of bone cancer. Her daughter-in-law, Barbara, and a few friends had banded together to find a way to honor her before she died. They had hoped to be able to fill a dream she'd often mentioned to them, which was to have lunch with me. Although they thought it impossible (the distance from California to Texas being a major challenge), they were willing to set out on the journey with their loved one and make it a possibility.

Through one of the secretaries at the WOF office, the date of April 11 was confirmed between Anne, Barbara, her pastor's wife, another friend, Mary Graham (president of Women of Faith) and me. We were scheduled to meet at the very nice restaurant in Neiman Marcus not far from my home and easily accessible by freeway to Anne's group, who had flown in the day before and stayed in a local hotel.

Mary and I had no idea what to expect. We got to Neiman's a bit early just in case we needed to hurry through lunch for Anne's sake. Our reservations were for eleven o'clock, when the restaurant first opened, and as we walked up to the receptionist at the front desk we spotted a waitress we knew. After visiting with her a few minutes, we asked if she could wait our table, because we knew her to be caring and attentive. We explained the very special nature of our lunch; so she immediately and lovingly agreed. Then there appeared before me a lovely brunette…the daughter-in-law of Anne. She was carrying a camera or two and sported the sweetest, broadest smile you can imagine, making her eyes dance.

She said, "Hi Luci. I'm Barbara, Anne's daughter-in-law. Thank you so much for meeting us today. We really appreciate you and Mary taking time for this."

I assured her it was no trouble at all; we were honored to have been asked.

"Do you mind if I take pictures of your first meeting Anne?"

she continued. "She's so excited about this. I already have pictures of our telling her what we were going to do, but we want to capture these next few moments too. Do you mind?"

"Absolutely not," I said. "Pictures are right up my alley! This is wonderful, Barbara. I don't mind any photos you want to take. Anything's fine with me."

At this point Anne hadn't yet arrived at the restaurant, so our waitress suggested we sit down at the table. No sooner had we taken a seat than Anne and two of her friends came around the corner. We all embraced as Barbara took pictures. It was an unforgettable moment. Anne is a beautiful woman, full of love and kindness and all the grace and charm in the world. Through our tears we talked briefly of the surprise element of the whole encounter and what an unforgettable gift that was to her from her loved ones.

For two full hours we ate lunch (even rich desserts!), laughed, cried, exchanged stories, engaged in meaningful, fun, rich conversation with each other, and not once did any of us want to leave. It was one of those times you hope will last forever! Even though Anne's strength was all but gone, exacerbated by the incessant pain she felt, she neither complained nor acted as if she needed to rush. She talked up a storm, and we were all mesmerized by her.

Barbara told us later that earlier that morning Anne had had a very difficult time getting out of bed, and they all debated whether or not she could go through with the plan. But on she came! And her friends sat amazed as they watched her energy, her appetite, and her joy increase as the time went on. Because of an idea that was carefully executed with love and tender care, a memory had been created that none of us will ever forget.

Those friends did something for Anne, and we did something for them, but God is the One who did the most for all of us. He lavished his grace on us in that brief moment of time. And as a result, we experienced the richest fellowship and love for him and one another that you can imagine, as if there were no cancer, no death, no tomorrow. As if we'd known one another for years. As if this day was the best day we'd ever had. As if nothing else mattered but our oneness in Christ and his grace.

Why do I tell you this story? Because Anne's attitude and mindset is a perfect example of living life fully—*in the moment*—no matter how she felt. What she had faced thus far, and what she might face in the future, did not distract her or us at all. She embraced joy for the moment, and we all drank it in. In so doing, we didn't miss the great gift our Father had for us. We received it.

Her friends took the time, went to the trouble, and made the effort to come. Anne had the spirit and spunk to trust God and give such a demanding trip her best effort. All we did was say yes. But none of us could have done what God did that day. It was beyond our power.

In a way, that meeting had an unexpected outcome. *She* wanted to meet *me*, but the truth was God wanted *me* to meet *her*. I was the one who received the refreshment. In Anne's dying condition, I've never experienced more life. In her receiving, I was given a meaningful gift. In her weakness, I was strengthened. In her laughter, I was moved to tears.

That's what happens when we allow joy to embrace us—the fullness of Christ's love fills our hearts to overflowing, which enables us to endure the pain. And it spills over into the lives of others.

My friend Sandy Lough finds herself in what could be called a joyless place. A few months ago her husband, Stuart, learned he has an inoperable brain tumor. The prognosis gives them no encouragement. Nevertheless, Sandy has chosen to let joy embrace her in the suffering that both she and Stuart feel.

A few days ago she wrote me a little note that said, in part, "I've never felt God's hand more strongly or lovingly than I have in all this painful process. I think the doctors think I'm in some sort of denial, but I do have a peace about it that I can't explain. [It passes understanding.] We're right where we're supposed to be, and we're going through this for a reason."

How would I be if Anne's cancer were mine? Or if I had a brain tumor? Or if my deepest loved one was suffering with one of these dilemmas? Would I let joy embrace me at all? I'd like to think so, but who knows until I'm actually in that spot? I can't be positive about my response, but I can be positive about what I believe. Anne, her friends, Sandy, and Stuart are vivid models of it:

Live one day at a time by savoring every moment.
Say yes to what leads to life, love, peace, and hope.

Embrace tests. They awaken new opportunities for us.

Give unselfishly of what you have and who you are.

By God's grace, have courage, patience, and forgiveness.

After Anne returned home to northern California, she wrote me the sweetest e-mail. It read, "Again you must know that God is so good to me—when I hurt he hugs me, and he never leaves my side. How unworthy am I that he would bless me by allowing me to be used for his glory. I felt for one moment that having lunch with one of God's chosen is one of my favorite rewards. Kind of a celestial moment."

Interestingly enough, Anne, that's *precisely* how I felt.

Life often leads us down paths we don't want to take. It gives us burdens we don't want to carry. It forces a change we don't want to make. We have to respond whether we like it or not. But the end result brings something out of us we'd never learn on an easier path. God's ways are not our ways. They're better and higher than our ways. Moses said it correctly hundreds of years ago: "Respond to the greatness of our God! The Rock: His works are perfect, and the way He works is fair and just; a God you can depend upon, no exceptions, a straight-arrow God" (Deuteronomy 32:3–4 MSG).

↺ *O God of joy, thank you for the celestial moments of life—the ones that leave us breathless, blessed, and believing. In those moments, we know we are truly in your presence, and we are humbled and oh so grateful. Amen.*

Embracing the Book
Patsy Clairmont
.ᕑ ✳ ᕑ.

Your Book is a lamp to my feet and a light for my path.
(PSALM 119:105, ADAPTED)

*W*ho or what do you enjoy embracing? Your sweetheart? A child? Fido? Fluffy? A hot fudge sundae? A goose-down pillow?

On my embracing priorities list, right after my hubby and my grandchildren, is wrapping my hands tenderly around the cover of a book. Well, not any book. I'm not much on the study of say, *Reptiles Roaming in Russia*, or *The Rigors of Rowing on the Riviera*, or *The Repair of Refrigeration Systems in Rwanda*, but give me a copy of *Huckleberry Finn* or *Pride and Prejudice*, and I'm a happy girl. I especially love sitting deep in a cushioned chair, a frothy cup of something carmel-y at my fingertips, embracing a copy of oh, say, *Jesus: Life Coach* by Laurie Beth Jones. And while comfort is not necessary to flip pages, for me it's definitely preferred, although I've stood in many a line and read my way to the cashier. And there's nothing more fun than partaking in a book that I know friends are reading as well, so at book's end I have a savvy group with whom to share thoughts.

Luci, as in Swindoll, is a constant source of book inspiration to me, because her reading menu is so varied. I'm always asking her what her current read is and usually I'm surprised at her choice, because it's something I didn't even know existed. The last one was about brains, which of course was out of my hemisphere. Luci embraces books on art, architecture, and Africa, just to name a few. She has an amazing library that fills my senses with delight and challenges me to read in a wider circle.

Because we Porch Pals (WOF speakers) spend so much time in transit on our way to conferences, we always carry books with us for the flights. We look like a traveling bookstore as we each dig into our bags and pull forth our latest treasures, and we're always checking out each other's current choices.

Actually, we are all well-rounded—as readers, I mean. Yet we all have leanings toward things that most interest us, subjects that are easy for us to embrace.

For instance, Thelma Wells is our motivational reader. She enjoys books that will add sparkle to her personal development. Nicole Johnson is our mystery reader—she loves a well-woven tale of intrigue and suspense. Sheila Walsh is our researcher, who hugs on books that turn Greek and Hebrew into applicable insights. Luci Swindoll is our artisan and takes pleasure in paintings from around the globe throughout history. Marilyn Meberg and I love a well-told tale—we are novel. Just kidding, but we do love novels, and because of our shared interests, Marilyn and I regularly resource each other for new selections.

I'm personally not much on kissy-face escapades (in book form, that is), which is why I was enthralled with the beautifully woven tale of love in Francine Rivers's, *Redeeming Love*. Based on the Old Testament story of Hosea, Francine stirs not only the issues of sacrificial love, faithfulness, and forgiveness, but she looks tenderly at shame.

Another novelist who has grown in her craft and ranks high on my chart is Liz Curtis Higgs. Her series set in Scotland is well researched, tastefully romantic, and full of surprises. I'm into twists and turns. I don't want to be able to figure out what's going to happen next—surprise me! Liz does.

I also love children's books. I am an *Anne of Green Gables* fan, as well as *Emily of New Moon*. The author of those and many more in the series is L. M. Montgomery, a pastor's wife from Prince Edward Island. Holly Hobby has done a great job on the *Toot and Puddle* series, both with her winsome stories on friendship, and her heartwarming illustrations. And Barbara Parks keeps me in stitches with her extensive collection about Junie B. Jones, a precocious little girl bursting with opinions that she constantly feels led to share. (I wonder if Junie and I are related?)

I'm a Charles Spurgeon fan, as well as an Oswald Chambers groupie. Ken Gire's work is, for me, like ladling cool water from a deep well—spiritually refreshing. And Henri Nouwen challenges me to think more introspectively and meditatively.

I think books in leather are sexy. OK, maybe not, but I do

appreciate a fine cover, quality paper, and sizable print. A well-designed book is a joy to embrace. For Christmas one year, Luci gave me an exquisite, gold-tooled, leather edition of *Sister Wendy's Art Guide*. It is a pleasure to hold and browse through.

OK, enough about my reading; I'll call a few friends and see what they are rifling through:

Luci Swindoll (author/friend) is currently reading *Pictures and Tears* (Elkins), *Why Art Cannot be Taught* (Elkins), and *Blink* (Gladwell). Her favorite book is *The Worst Journey in the World* (Garrard), which tells the trials of traveling to Antarctica.

Mary Graham (president WOF/friend) is also reading *Blink* (Gladwell) about intuition and a book on working together called *Teammates* (about a group of guys who played for the Red Sox many years ago and maintained their friendship more than fifty years after.) It's by David Halberstam, an historian.

Jan Silvious (author/friend) is reading *Don't Waste Your Life* (Piper), and *Strong Women, Soft Hearts* (Rinehart).

Lana Bateman (Women of Faith chaplain/friend) just finished *O Ye Jigs and Juleps* (Hudson) and *Miss Julia Speaks Her Mind* (Ross).

I haven't always been a reader; in fact, I didn't become one until I was an adult, a desperate adult. Once I discovered the joy of hugging a book, I've been knee-deep in volumes of reading material ever since. And the one Book that I return to again and again has been the Bible. It is the most important book in my library, and I know my friends would be the first to agree wholeheartedly concerning their libraries. For while we have enjoyed the pens of others, our hearts have only been transformed by God's truths found in his Book. We've been encouraged by others but redeemed by Christ.

I would have to say my favorite book in the Bible is Genesis. Perhaps because I love beginnings and hearing how God established the world. Or maybe it's because of the architectural wonder of the ark, or the arduous life journey of Abraham, or the trials of Joseph. During times of conflict I've revisited Sarah and Hagar and have been reminded of the cost of unforgiveness that can impact generations. And I have walked through Joseph's life amazed at the strength and grace God gave him in the midst of injustice, slander, and cruel attempts to dishonor him.

But then again I also love Proverbs for its in-your-face practicality, and Philippians for its joy-filled encouragement regardless of life's vicissitudes, and Isaiah for its holy imagery, and the Psalms for their divine music, and John for its tender accounts of Christ, and, and, and . . . OK, OK, I like the whole Book because it helps me become a whole person and gives me hope for future generations.

I find freedom by embracing truth, and that truth is often revealed to me through the written words of others. So I invite you to join me in a cup of something frothy or icy, call Fido and Fluffy to your side or lap, sink into your favorite chair, position your pillow, and open up a good book.

♄ *Father, I praise you for the incredible Book you have written for me to follow. I embrace its teachings and store them in my heart as my source of joy. Thank you for your Book, Lord. Amen.*

God's Gift Bearers

SHEILA WALSH

ა❋ ა

To everything there is a season,
   a time for every purpose under heaven.
A time to be born and a time to die;
A time to plant, and a time to pluck what is planted,
A time to kill and a time to heal;
A time to break down and a time to build up;
A time to weep, and a time to laugh;
A time to mourn and a time to dance;
A time to cast away stones and a time to gather stones;
A time to embrace, and a time to refrain from embracing;
A time to gain, and a time to lose;
A time to keep, and a time to throw away,
A time to tear, and a time to sew;
A time to keep silence and a time to speak;
A time to love, and a time to hate;
A time of war, and a time of peace.
                     (ECCLESIASTES 3:1–8 NKJV)

The book of Ecclesiastes is not one of the most widely read books in the Old Testament, but many people are familiar with the above passage. The text as a whole is often criticized as being fatalistic and negative, and some evangelical scholars suggest it contains the writings of a man far apart from God. It sounds to me more like a man reflecting on his life and the futility of so many of the things he once pursued. The authorship is not absolutely clear, but most of the evidence points to Solomon as the writer. Chapter 1 introduces him as "the son of David, king in Jerusalem."

Accepting Solomon's authorship, Ecclesiastes was most likely written toward the end of his life when he had turned away from some of his poor choices and pursuit of foreign wives. It seems to me that there is a sad wisdom in his words, a wisdom birthed as a man examines the consequences of rebellion and sin, of time lost that can never be relived. The familiar words in chapter 3 have impacted countless lives in every generation.

In the mid-1960s, the Byrds—the American equivalent of the Beatles—had a number one hit with their version of Bob Seeger's classic song "Turn, Turn, Turn." The lyrics are based on our passage from Ecclesiastes 3. I think it's significant that the song has been recorded many times by secular and gospel artists alike. I recorded it myself in the 1980s. There is such truth contained in this acknowledgment of the joys and sorrows of life, the give and take, the hopes and fears of every man, woman, and child who has ever lived. Anyone who has walked through a dark night knows that there are times when every one of us needs to be embraced, even in an unlikely setting.

Life had been pretty nutty around our house in December 2004, as I'm sure it was around yours at that time of year.

Christian was so excited about Christmas, and he was turning eight too. He had decided to have his party at the house rather than the usual pizza place or laser-tag; so we would have twenty-four pairs of happy feet running around. We were also hosting the Women of Faith staff Christmas party at our house, which meant eighty-five more pairs of happy feet.

So I had decided to take an hour away from my to-do list and have a pedicure. I melted into the seat, plopped my feet into a bath of fragrant warm water and closed my eyes. I resisted the nail technician's insistence that everyone should choose red polish at Christmas.

"Miss Sheila, you must wear red; it's the holidays!"

"That's not in the Bible," I replied, giving her my purple polish.

"Ah, you crazy!" she replied, not for the first time.

I began to drift away when I heard someone say, "You look just like Sheila Walsh." I opened my eyes and turned to the woman who was now sitting in the chair beside me.

"Oh, you are Sheila Walsh!" she said. We chatted for a few moments, and she told me that she had attended a couple of our conferences and how much they had helped her. We talked about our children, and she told me that she has three young ones.

"They must be excited," I said.

"Christmas will be different for us this year," she replied. "My husband died of brain cancer."

"I'm so sorry," I said. "When did he die?"

"Yesterday."

We sat in silence for a few moments. I was stunned at the immediacy of this loss. My heart ached for her and for her children.

"Our church has been wonderful in every way," she said. "I have seen God's love in action."

I told her of God's amazing faithfulness to my mom when she was left with three children to raise after my father's death. God's presence was so evident as we sat together, two women with their feet in tubs of hot water, their hearts in the hands of the King of kings, holding hands across a tray of nail polish.

I was finished first and went to wash my hands. When I got back she was gone, but there was a note for me. She wrote that even as she drove to the salon that morning she had prayed for peace and protection and thanked God that he sat us next to each other. "I just needed a touch of God with skin on."

I tell this story for two reasons. One, I covet your prayers for this mom and her three children. Her name is Gina. I don't know the children's names, but our Father does.

Second, that day was a reminder that God never takes his eyes off us; he sees us and cares about us. He saw this exhausted, heartbroken woman as she drove to a nail salon, a brief respite before the evening's wake for her beloved husband, and he sat her beside a sister in God's family with skin on.

It reminded me, too, that we don't know what is going on in the lives of those we brush shoulders with every day. Only God can give us eyes to see and ears to hear and the grace to be the fragrance of Christ where life has turned sour. Often, those who have experienced a terrible loss have the added wound of feeling as if they have suddenly become a social pariah and people are avoiding them. It's hard to know what to do or say when we meet someone who has gone through a great tragedy. I have discovered that there is no right thing to say, but we can always give ourselves. At times a warm embrace, a shared silent moment, or a few shed tears means more than eloquent words.

It may seem strange to talk about such painful issues in a book on joy, but I believe there is a mystery at work here. When Adam and Eve walked with God in the garden, one of the hallmarks of their lives was oneness with each other and God. Satan's nature then and now is to bring division and isolation, to make men, women, and children carry their burdens alone. We are invited to be part of God's antidote to that demonic poison and reach out with the love and compassion of Christ.

We have the joy of inviting the Holy Spirit to empower us to be gift bearers, to embrace the lonely, wounded ones with the heart of our Father.

> What can I give him, poor as I am?
> If I were a shepherd, I would bring a lamb;
> If I were a wise man, I would do my part;
> Yet what I can I give him: give my heart.
> —CHRISTINA ROSSETTI

ॐ *Father, I ask in Jesus's name that you would give me eyes to see and ears to hear the hurting ones around me. Give me your grace to reach out and embrace them in your name. For Jesus's sake, amen.*

There's Nothing Like a Mother's Embrace ... Except the Father's

BARBARA JOHNSON

✻

The eternal God is thy refuge,
and underneath are the everlasting arms.
(DEUTERONOMY 33:27 KJV)

*M*y friend Sue was a nervous wreck when her son, Sam, headed off to college in Houston, Texas, a thousand miles away from the family's home in Florida. Sam was a bright kid, but Houston seemed like such a huge place, and those thousand miles standing between her and her only son might as well have been a million, Sue thought.

As she helped him move into his dorm room, Sue thought up reasons why she needed to linger. But eventually the time came for her to climb into the minivan and head for home.

When she finally drove away, leaving Sam standing alone on the sidewalk, she smiled brightly and waved good-bye. Then, as soon as she was out of sight, she stopped in a parking lot and cried like a baby. By the time she had made her way back to

Florida, she had gone through an industrial-size box of tissues and filled God's ear with so many urgent and heartfelt prayers, she was sure he must be sick of the sound of her whiny, tear-stretched voice.

Sue was traveling around the country with me to Women of Faith conferences at that time, helping at my book table. At our next venue, she mentioned to Lisa Pierre, who lives in Houston, that Sam would be going to school there. Lisa is one of the talented worship leaders who thrill Women of Faith audiences with wonderful praise music. She has a powerful voice and an enthusiastic heart for God. And she's a mom herself to teenagers Josef and Kamri.

"If there's anything I can do for you while your son's in Houston, just let me know," Lisa told Sue, reaching for a pen and paper. "Here's my phone number. If you need anything—if Sam needs anything—you call me."

"Oh, Lisa," Sue said, feeling a sudden rush of relief sweep over her, "it makes me feel so much better to know you're there and that you're willing to help Sam if he needs it. I pray it will never happen, but, you know, if Sam ever got really sick or hurt and ended up in a hospital . . ."

"Just call me," Lisa said. "Or have Sam call me. I'll be the 'mama arms' holding him until you can get there."

"And Lisa," Sue continued, "Sam's a good boy, but you know, even good kids make bad decisions sometimes . . ."

"I can find the jail," Lisa said, laughing. "I'll hold his hand through the bars until you show up."

Every time Lisa and Sue were together at Women of Faith, Lisa would ask how Sam was doing. The conversation would end with Lisa saying, "Don't forget. You just call me, and if Sam ever needs my help in Houston, I'll be there."

A couple of years went by like this. Then I was diagnosed with cancer and had to stop traveling with the Women of Faith tour, which meant Sue stopped traveling with the tour too. She didn't see Lisa until another two years had passed. Then, while she was attending a Women of Faith conference somewhere, she made a point of seeking out Lisa to tell her the good news.

"Well, Lisa, I'm happy to tell you you're relieved of substitute-mama duty," she said. "Sam is graduating this month."

Then Sue showed Lisa that her number was still stored on Sue's cell phone. "I've had three different cell phones since you first gave me your number, Lisa, but I've always made sure to copy your number over onto the new phone. It meant so much to me that you were ready to help my son if there was an emergency."

Recently Sue showed her son a picture of Lisa. "You don't know this beautiful woman," she said, "but for four years she's been on standby, ready to run to you anytime you needed help. If anything bad had happened to you while you were in Houston, Lisa's arms would have been mine, holding you until I could get there."

Sam looked at Lisa's picture and smiled. "Pretty cool, Mom. But . . . why would she do that, when she doesn't even know me?"

"She's a mom, and she understands how powerful a mother's embrace can be when hard times hit," Sue said.

I've had the honor of mothering young people who were not my own children, and I believe that the joy of *giving* that kind of support is surely as great as the comfort of having it unexpectedly bestowed when you're the one in need. For me, the most memorable time came when a mother from far away called me frantically one Saturday morning and asked me to rescue her son, who lived near our town in Southern California.

The woman and her husband had returned earlier than planned from an out-of-town trip and had found in their mail a tape cassette from their son telling them he had AIDS and that he was going to take his own life. They felt certain he had thought that by the time they heard the tape (which was supposed to be several days later), he would have already committed suicide.

They had tried to reach him by phone to no avail. Now they were hundreds of miles away and, they needed help for their son.

"Would you find him, Barb?" the woman asked. "We don't know who else to call."

I followed her directions to her son's address, and in a dark and dank apartment that I first mistook for a laundry room, I found him. Then I did for him what his own mother would have done. I talked to him, listened to him, and encouraged him. Over the next few months, Bill and I made sure he had food to eat, a decent place to live, and a network of professional and support-group resources. But most importantly, whenever I was with him, I hugged him with a mother's arms and told him that God loved him—and I did too.

There's something about a mother's embrace that provides relief, comfort, encouragement, and love like nothing else. In difficult times, even the strongest adults long for the feel of their mothers' arms wrapping around them. Throughout history there have been stories about warriors wounded in battle or adults injured in terrible accidents who, as death closed in on them, cried out for their mothers.

What power we have in our mothering arms! What a gift God has given us mothers to provide solace and refuge to those around us—whether we're comforting our own children or someone else's—or reaching out to another mother who knows that only someone who's stumbled along her same difficult journey can understand what she has had to bear.

I've traveled the country, telling audiences how God's great comfort and joy were the only things that could possibly have brought me through the hardships I've known—the death of two sons, the homosexuality of another son, and most recently, the death of my husband. And every place I've spoken, women come up to me, often teary-eyed, needing a hug from someone who's walked the pathway they suddenly find themselves on.

The next time you give someone a hug of encouragement, imagine the love of God filling your heart so that it overflows from your heart and moves out through your arms to soak right into the person you're embracing. Whether you're physically fit or you have what one of my friends calls "flab wings" above your elbows, you have power in those arms.

And that's not all. Our arms are multilingual. Like music, a mother's embrace transcends any language barriers—and not just international languages but languages of the heart. Without a word, a mother's hug can say so many things:

"I love you."

"I believe in you. I know you can do it."

"Congratulations!"

"I understand."

But the most sought-after message of a mother's arms is the same one our Father God extends to us when he embraces us in his everlasting arms of love. It's the message we long to hear throughout our lives, from the time we fall down as toddlers and seek Mom's solace as we wail about our skinned knees right up to the moment when we take our last earthly breath and step into eternity. It's the reassurance that everything's going to be OK.

A mother's arms carry the message of God's love wrapped up with the gift of hope, divine joy, and strengthened by the promise of eternal life. It's as though our arms can say what God says to us whenever life sends us reeling: "There, there. It's all right. I'm here. We'll just cry together a little while, then I'll help you get back on your feet. We'll work on putting one foot in front of the other until you're able to face whatever comes next. And if it's something you can't handle alone, remember I'm here for you."

ᴄ Heavenly Father, strong and kind, thank you for your constant presence in my life and for your strong arms of faith that hold me when I hurt and lift me when I fall. Amen.

PART 3

～

Joy Whispers

If You'll Talk, He'll Listen

THELMA WELLS

ぬ ✳ ぬ

Lord, teach us to pray. (LUKE 11:1 NIV)

*M*en ought to always pray." You may ask, "How can you pray when you don't know what prayer is?" Here's one definition: Prayer is the heart's sincere desire unspoken or expressed. Prayer is communicating with God, sharing with God your dreams and desires, listening to God for answers, calling on God when you are in distress, thanking God for his goodness to you. Prayer is opening up and expressing to God exactly what you feel about a situation. Yes, it might even be yelling at God as you try to understand your heartaches and disappointments.

After leading a young man in a prayer to receive Jesus as his Savior, I suggested to him that he begin to pray every day. His comment was, "But I don't know how to pray."

I responded, "Do you know how to talk?"

A little shocked at my response, he answered, "Sure!"

"Well, if you can talk, you can pray." Just open your mouth and tell God whatever you need to tell him, or ask him whatever you need to know. It's so much easier talking to God than to another person. A person may misinterpret what you're saying. God never misinterprets. In fact, he already knows what you need before you ask. Therefore, you're safe talking to God about anything. He will hear and answer your prayers.

God's answers are always for our good. Maybe you're thinking, *I asked God for this or that, and he hasn't answered me yet.* That's not always true. God answers our prayers in his own time, because *his* time is not *our* time. God answers prayers in several ways. Sometimes he says yes. Sometimes he says no. Sometimes he says wait.

Talking to God is like talking to a good parent. If a child asks a parent for something that will do the child good, the parent may say yes. If a child asks a parent for something harmful to that child, the parent may say no. If the child asks a parent for something the child is not ready for, even though it may be good for them, the answer may be wait. God is the best Father we can have.

One thing I've discovered about prayer is that usually my prayers involve other people. Maybe I'm praying for a person's physical healing, but that person has decided they want the ultimate healing, death. That happened with two of my friends. God has said that the days of our lives are numbered, and only he knows when our time on this earth is over. It would be futile for me to get angry with God for not answering our prayers the way we wanted, because he knows the end from the beginning. He allowed them the privilege of understanding that their time was about over, and they both died with dignity, leaving legacies of lives well lived. God was ready for them. We can't always understand God's timing, but we *can* know that he never makes a mistake. Perhaps I'm praying for a loved one to be saved, but she refuses to accept Jesus as her Savior. There might be a broken relationship that I want mended, but the other person is rejecting the relationship. God understands all the people and circumstances in our prayers and works things out according to what is good for all of us.

Although we can't understand God's timing, we *can* understand the conditions for answered prayer. God has a master plan for our prayer lives that includes our attitudes and our reasons for praying.

We must acknowledge God. Our acknowledgment of God honors and respects God's name, his character, his integrity, his sovereignty, and his power. Do you remember that the prayer Jesus taught his disciples to pray—we call it the Lord's Prayer—begins with "Our Father, which art in heaven, hallowed be Thy name"? Acknowledging God as hallowed or holy opens the door for him to communicate with his children.

We must support our prayers by the intercession of Jesus and the Holy Spirit. The Son of God, Jesus, has the position as our heavenly intercessor with God. This means that he is seated at the right hand of the throne of God praying for us to his Father. I like to think that when I pray, Jesus says something like this to

God: "Father, Thelma is in need of peace in her spirit. You promised that you would give her perfect peace if she keeps her mind on me. Her mind is set on me because I see her studying your Word, applying your principles, learning your precepts, and recognizing your lordship. Please, give her instant peace." I believe, right then and there, the peace of God comes over me, and I calm down and begin to think more clearly.

Jesus is our High Priest and has direct access to God. As our great High Priest, Jesus listens and attends to our confessions. In fact, Jesus is the only priest, pastor, minister, prophet, or bishop who can do us everlasting good. When we pray, therefore, we need to pray in the name of Jesus. We can be assured that when we do, Jesus attends to us and prays for us. We never pray alone. We pray with our great High Priest. Hebrews 4:14–16 reads,

> Seeing then that we have a great high priest, that is passed into the heavens, Jesus the Son of God, let us hold fast our profession. For we have not an high priest which cannot be touched with the feeling of our infirmities; but was in all points tempted like as we are, yet without sin. Let us therefore come boldly unto the throne of grace, that we may obtain mercy, and find grace to help in time of need. (KJV)

This just sums it up. When you've got Jesus praying for you, you don't need anybody else. Hallelujah!

I am blown away by the orderliness of God. Not only has he

provided for us a heavenly intercessor in Jesus, he has provided for us an earthly intercessor, the Holy Spirit. God anticipated that we would plead weakness or ignorance or give some excuse about how we can't pray and don't know how to pray. So the all-knowing God provided for us an earthly advocate to live inside us to guide us in our prayers. Listen to this:

> The Spirit also helpeth our infirmities for we know not what we should pray for as we ought; but the Spirit itself maketh intercession for us with groanings which cannot be uttered. And he that searcheth the hearts knows what is the mind of the Spirit, because he maketh intercession for the saints according to the will of God. (Romans 8:26–27 KJV)

The Holy Spirit always interprets our prayers to the Father in accordance to the will of God, and he helps us understand God's will for our lives. When we accept Jesus as our personal Lord and Savior, the Holy Spirit comes to live in our hearts. This Holy Spirit of God is the person who convicts us when we do wrong, comforts us when we are sad, and guides us in what we do. The Holy Spirit is our advocate in heaven. Wow! We have two great, high, and holy advocates always working in unison to bring us into the presence and glory of God our Father.

If you have been feeling alone and not able to pray, trust the fact that you have Jesus and the Holy Spirit overshadowing any insecurity you may have about praying to God. You have the most potent, powerful beings in the universe on your side, making your situation known and resolved by the Father.

If you don't know God as your Creator, Jesus as your Savior, and the Holy Spirit as your Guide, this is a great time to ask him into your heart and to become Lord of your life. You can pray this prayer right now, wherever you are:

Jesus, because I know you are real and you care about me, please come into my heart and become my Lord and Savior. I believe that God raised Jesus from the dead and that you, Jesus, live in the world today. I want to be able to fully depend on you to help me in my time of need and to rejoice with me when I'm happy. I receive you as Lord. I want the Holy Spirit to live inside me, helping me with all my issues. Thank you for accepting me, because I fully accept you. Amen.

Your wondering days are over! Jesus came into your life according to Romans 10:9 that says, "If you confess with your mouth the Lord Jesus and believe in your heart that God has raised Him from the dead, you will be saved" (NKJV).

Now you have all the rights and privileges of all God's children and the promise of life eternal.

⁓ *Our Father in heaven, we praise you, and we worship you for we know that you alone are Almighty God, ruler of the universe, and the source of our joy. Amen.*

Pitcher This

PATSY CLAIRMONT

৵ ✳ ৵

The sword of the LORD and Gideon! (JUDGES 7:20 NKJV)

I started out life as a shouter. Didn't mean to be, but my pitch could have shattered pitchers. Years ago, in an attempt to be more socially acceptable, I practiced lowering my volume by whispering, which I soon found out also annoyed some people. "Whadyasay?" "Are you talking to me?" "If you have something to say, say it!"

I think I developed my loudness because I grew up with a hearing-impaired mother. I knew in her presence to speak up and enunciate clearly, unless I didn't want mom to hear and then, even with her hearing aid off and my back to her, Mom somehow could decipher my coded mumbles. Go figure.

After years of hearing-aid apparatuses of every imaginable size, Mom had an experimental surgery that restored her hearing. They replaced the smallest bone in our bodies, a tiny horse-shoe configuration that nests in the ear canal. In fact, it was so effective that after her surgery Mom was *too* sensitive to sound, and we were all tiptoeing around her. Ticking clocks were replaced with silent ones, the television volume was lowered dramatically, and doors were carefully closed so they didn't slam and rattle her. And for heaven's sake, we didn't run the garbage disposal when she was in the kitchen unless you wanted to be part of the minced meat. Mom's supersonic hearing necessitated my personal need for volume control. Shhh.

Whispering, while considered polite and preferred in certain situations, is absolutely rude in others. To whisper can suggest to some people that we are saying something secretive, seductive, or even scandalous. Whispering can accentuate paranoia, separate friends, and stir speculations. And yet whispering is the law in libraries and intensive care units. And what's more tender than newlyweds whispering sweet nothings to each other? I don't even want to know what they're saying, thank you.

I wonder if whispering began as a cover-up attempt when Eve bit into the apple? Hmm, I'd rather believe it began as she and Adam quietly made their way around the garden to check on the animals before bedtime. Can you imagine peeking in on the zebras, crocodiles, and lions? I'd definitely be lowering my voice.

Have you watched or participated in parental whispers over a baby's crib? It's joyous sounds as parents bless their little ones, wishing them sweet dreams and restful hours . . . so that the child might flourish and the parents might recover.

Have you noticed when you lower your voice that others tend to follow suit? It's as if whispering is, well, contagious. I have followed the quiet lead of others and then in hushed tones finally inquired, "Why are we whispering?" Somehow whispering seems the appropriate response to others who are using their softest sounds, like children's host Mister Rogers, the darling of gentleness. (Didn't you want that man with his tender heart and whispery voice to live in your neighborhood? I did.)

There are many things in nature that whisper, like a grove of evergreens. Lean in sometime, if you haven't in a while, and hear the gentle lullaby of breezes through pine branches. The soothing sound is comforting while the ancient fragrance that wafts and then settles on everything in its path is deeply refreshing. It seems to untangle my nerves and quiet my racing thoughts.

It's as if I hear God's voice in the wind—whispering, "Be still and know that I am God" (Psalm 46:10 NIV). We are told that one day the trees will applaud; so I should not be surprised until that glorious day that they speak of him in holy hushes.

Another whispering place is next to a brook. You may at times have to stoop down and listen closely to catch the words, but they are there—swishing sounds like angel wings, sounds that replenish the soul. Brooks invite stillness and stir longings for heavenly exchanges.

Recently, in one of my rare aerobic moments, I took a long walk in an attempt to convince the pouch on my tummy to slide down and slip out my sneakers, when I came across a blossoming rose garden in a neighbor's yard. Cloistered near the profusion of flowers was a statue of a girl carrying a basket, as if she were out gathering the bounty of the yard. No, the statue did not speak. Whew! Gratefully, she was stone silent. But the roses' gentle giggles caught my ear, and their sweet fragrance reminded me of the One who tucked the perfume deep within their petals.

In our neighborhood there are scores of mourning doves, birds that truly use their indoor voices outside, unlike the annoying blue jays nearby, who in amplified tones make their presence constantly known. "See me! See me!" they seem to screech, all the while flaunting their size and flashy blues. In contrast, when I hear the faint coos of the doves among the branches, I wonder what thoughtful things they must be saying to each other. They are always in pairs and seldom seemed ruffled.

Have you noticed how difficult it is to fight in whispers? My volume always goes up when I'm ruffled and gives me away—for some reason I think I can't make my point quietly. I guess I'm afraid the recipient won't get it if I'm not stern and stereo. I think woofers and tweeters are helpful in winning a war. Although . . .

That certainly was not the case for Gideon. I mean it wasn't that Gideon wasn't shouting. He was, as were all his three hundred men, but measure that against the one hundred twenty thousand enemies they were facing, and Gideon's shouts suddenly seem more like whispers. Gideon and his army were not only outnumbered; they came without weapons and attacked at night. And they didn't come equipped with microphones, cell phones, not even a megaphone. What they had were horns and lit torches that they dropped inside of pitchers. Uh-huh, pitch-ers. If this had been a Betty Crocker cook-off, pitchers would have seemed appropriate, but war?

Yet Gideon and his soldiers blew the horns, broke the pitch-ers, and shouted into the night, "The sword of the Lord and Gideon!" (Judges 7:20).

And they actually won! Who'd a thunk it? Why did they win? Perhaps the Midianites had a horn phobia. Or maybe break-ing pottery broke them up. Hardly. No, it was because Gideon lis-tened to the instructions of the Lord and then obeyed him.

Gideon had grown in obedience. That gives me hope. He actually began his military career reluctantly. No, it was more than that; Gideon was downright resistant. He couldn't believe the Lord wanted him to be a leader. He knew he wasn't leader material. And when the angel of the Lord greeted Gideon with, "The LORD is with you, you mighty man of valor," Gideon was stunned and stumped (Judges 6:12 NKJV).

Gideon knew he wasn't a mighty man of valor, and he had seen no signs of the Lord being for his people, much less being on Gideon's side. I think it's interesting that Gideon determined God's presence or lack thereof based on his circumstances. I've done that too. Gratefully God is longsuffering toward us. Why, he could have turned Gideon into a horn or me into a stone girl in a garden, but instead he generously meets with us and con-tinues to reassure us of his ongoing presence, his perfect plan, and his provisional power.

No wonder the Lord's whispers become our shouts. "The

sword of the LORD and of Gideon!" "The sword of the LORD and of Patsy!" Oh, I know I won't have to go to war against the Midianites, but I fight battles every day, don't you?

Sometimes, like Gideon, I am my own worst enemy. For even when I hear the Savior's voice in the wind of the pines, or detect his fragrance in a rose, or experience his refreshment at the brook, or am reminded to gently coo as a dove instead of squawk as a blue jay, I am resistant. "Could you speak louder?" I ask of God. "How do I know this is you, O Lord? Could you send me a notarized fax for my files? Oh, yes, in duplicate please . . . with a photo and your current phone number."

I am encouraged when I listen to the conversations between the Lord and Gideon. I am reminded that the Lord understands our frailty and hesitancy, he is not offended by our doubts or questions, he makes himself known in many ways, and when he asks us to come to the battlefield, he goes with us.

Are you battle weary? Feeling insecure? Do your enemies outnumber you? Does God's counsel seem ineffective for your situation? If so, remember trembling Gideon, who lived up to the Lord's pronouncement: "You mighty man of valor!"

Just know it's scary for most of us to trust God when he whispers instructions in our ear, but it is pure joy when we obey and witness his smashing victory!

✤ *Come to me in whispers, O Lord, because I could not survive your shouts. But please come! I need your quiet presence, your mighty power, your gentle comfort. Amen.*

Latitude of Longing

NICOLE JOHNSON

ళ ✻ ళ

A longing fulfilled is sweet to the soul.
(PROVERBS 13:19 NIV)

A longing is the heart whispering to the mind that we human beings were made for more than this world has to offer us. It might be easy to believe that these whisperings are more about dissatisfaction, but I believe they are from God. These yearnings and hungers that will not be fully satisfied on earth speak very clearly to me of heaven. Sociologist Peter Berger calls these whisperings "signals of transcendence," and Philip Yancey calls them "rumors of another world." Whatever we call them, we only glimpse them briefly.

In the winter of 2002 I got a really good glimpse. A little band of friends and I got together for an expedition that would take us to the coolest part of the world, literally—Antarctica. It was summer there and the only time of year that a ship like ours can cross into its usually frozen waters. We all read up on this frozen continent before we went, and we came to know quite a bit, but we had no way to know that it was a trip that would change all of our lives by what we saw and experienced.

Inside my heart lives far more emotion and depth than I normally access. It would be overwhelming if I tried. But every once in a while, either through pain or joy, I get down into those layers of my heart. I will confess that I try to cherish these times, particularly when they are about deep joy. Something touches me that turns me upside down or inside out and makes me do something really crazy, like write bad poetry.

Now that may not sound so crazy to you because I'm a writer, but I am *not* a poet. Trust me, there is a big difference. I fancy myself having the soul of a poet without the talent, which means I can feel all the torturous emotions without having any reward, like producing brilliant verses. But when I am deeply moved, I often attempt to write poems.

I encourage myself, and actually others as well, to write *bad* poetry, because this takes the pressure off producing anything brilliant. I find the real value is in tapping into those deep layers and putting words around what I am feeling, that I might come to understand myself better, or catch one of those glimpses of heaven. If I am seeking to be profound or to write a *good* poem, that wrecks everything for me, and all those raw feelings are wasted. It's far better to *explore* them than *exploit* them.

When I meet the page as a poet, I don't write in complete sentences, and my words don't even have to make any sense to anyone. That sets me free to write the truth of what I feel or leave gaps where I have questions or confusion. The beauty of a poem, even a bad one, comes as much from what is *not* written as from what *is*. Like a watercolor that must use the color of the paper wisely, so must a poem use space intentionally. This usually means that much of the meaning of a poem remains hidden, except to the poet. And this is why many poets are poor. They're rich in spirit, of course, for they have mined the jewels in their hearts, treasuring them, instead of polishing and selling them.

So back to Antarctica. While we were there I was completely overcome by the grandeur and beauty of the continent. It awakened such longings in me, not unlike what I had experienced in Africa almost ten years before. Every day we would see something that would just stir our souls to the depths, or inspire us and bring sheer delight, like the penguins.

I had never seen such creatures of pure joy. I don't know if this is true or not, but with their funny little walks and their quirky characteristics, penguins appear so happy all the time. They seem carefree and so full of life. They aren't really birds, because they have no wingspan and don't fly as other birds, but as we figured out from watching them, they fly under water— they fly and fly and fly! It was so fun for us all to watch their delightful little antics, in the water and out, and try to capture it in a photo or two or ten, which was impossible—you really had to be there. Penguins have so much life and personality that we started naming people of whom they reminded us.

I can hardly even describe the excitement we felt passing our first iceberg. And then to put foot on land and hike to the top of a mountain—well, it was breathtaking! Why are there so few good words? I was filled with such awe to awaken each day to a solitary continent of frozen snow and ice that featured the bluest sky in the world. It was hard to believe that we were there, and almost as soon as we did believe, it was time to go home.

Then came the whispers of longing. "Why does this have to end? The world is so different here and so wild and rugged, yet it is peaceful beyond measure and quiet. How can I hold on to all that I feel without forgetting it?" I felt such sadness in leaving. As we prepared to leave and our trip came to a close, I remember saying to a close friend, "Who knew an iceberg could break your heart?"

Sometimes I don't open my heart to joy because I'm afraid of the pain. I'm afraid if I dive in as deep as I can go that I'm only setting myself up for loss and hurt. No one can deny that joy and pain are very closely connected, and perhaps they are even inseparable. When something, or even someone, brings great joy, this also has enormous potential to cause you pain. And the reverse is also true: where there is pain, usually there once was joy. So with joy being a mixed bag, sometimes I just don't open my heart. I'm not proud of that, but it's true.

In Antarctica, though, I forgot to be detached. I was captured by the wonder and the majesty, and I was writing and shooting pictures and making friends with penguins—enjoying my time, and then it was over. The joy was still there, but the pain started to set in as we began the voyage home. I started feeling things way down in those under layers, and I wasn't sure what to do. So

I began experimenting, playing around really, with words and lines and verses, trying to write a bad poem, or anything that would help me with all that I was feeling. I began to unpack the images and emotions with random, but descriptive words that felt as different as a thick paintbrush and a fine little pencil.

I'm sharing with you my bad poem. This is not the way it tumbled out of me; I worked to make it more presentable, but long after I'd found all my words. And coming back to it, to include it here, I wanted to work on it some more, but I resisted the urge to try to make it *better*, in favor of letting you see it as it was. I finished it three years ago, and it has become one of the most valuable things I brought home from the trip.

Latitude of Longing

A majestic mystery of mountains, ice and water
Holding all light in whiteness
Cradling all color in its forms
Radiating a warmth all its own

Hearts beat with uncharted excitement
The cold can freeze only the moments in time
Thrilling and threatening, delighting and daunting
A holy parade of nature's beautiful secrets

A continent extending her fickle welcome
Proudly inhospitable, desolate and desirous at once
A stubborn sun refuses to set, saving the best light for the night

Daring the lover to penetrate the inner circle
Will she refuse or embrace?

Icebergs—masters of subtext,
Holding their greatest depth underneath
A gliding show-and-tell of silent strength

Penguins—enthusiastic torpedoes,
Feathered with joy
Flying freely in thawing beauty
Celebrating the spectrum of summer

Peaks—fierce glory and frozen splendor,
Rugged and impolite
Reflected brilliance, sharp enough to cut the eyes
Matte gray mist, soft enough to soothe the mind
Words find themselves lost and confused

Oh latitude of longing
You cannot satisfy what you stir
Mutely pointing to the Greater
Ever reminding of the Higher
Perpetuating the yearning
Kindling dreams of returning.

೨   *O Majestic Father, I long to be in your presence, to taste the sweetness of your joy, to rest in the quietness of your Spirit. Come to me, O Lord, through the longings of my heart. Amen.*

Unspeakable Joy

MARY GRAHAM

᳁ ✳ ᳁

Be still, and know that I am God.
(PSALM 46:10, NIV)

*I*n the early 1980s, I had the wonderful and exciting experience of working with a team of my peers to help establish a ministry on university campuses in the Soviet Union. We spent long days and drawn-out nights sitting in middle seats on planes, trains, and automobiles. We skipped meals and lived on protein bars and M&Ms. We slept in bad hotels and rode on elevators that I assume were made in China before the Great Wall was built. And we created memories we'll never forget.

It was all unforgettable, but what I remember most are the students we met, the long conversations and heartfelt encounters we had with them, watching them consider Christ, and seeing many coming to a saving knowledge of a personal relationship with him. As they ultimately came to faith, it was amazing to realize all that it meant for their lives and futures. As with anyone, knowing Christ changed everything. We took many trips to their country and fell in love with the Natashas, Olgas, Svetlanas, and others we met there. Just thinking about it brings back the memories.

Because it was before the Berlin Wall came down in East Germany and during the era that the Communist Party held full sway over the people, it was a bit dangerous to do the work we did. We were careful at every turn, not wanting to tempt fate in any way, but asking God to help us be brave and faithful in taking his love and grace to that part of the world. We saw the opportunity before us and didn't want to miss it.

My parents were completely opposed to my going, so I wrote them a postcard every day (as if they would receive even one of them before I got home!). In time, they came around to being so interested in what we were doing and waiting with eagerness to hear the stories of the girls we met that they seemed like a part of our ministry.

When we arrived on that first trip, we went to the building where the English majors studied. We sat down trying to look inconspicuous. As they heard our discussion (and I'm sure recognized that we were aliens from another planet), they were eager to engage us in conversation. Even though they had studied English all their lives, they had never met people who spoke it as their native language. We later learned that they were eager to get to know us because they wanted to learn American slang. They later learned we were just as eager to know them, because we wanted to teach them something much more life changing.

We spent days wandering around the streets of Leningrad, walking and talking. It wasn't always safe to have conversation inside buildings; so for security reasons, we mostly talked outside. I've never walked so much in my life. "Madee" they would say to me in their heavy Slavic accents, "It tis not far. Perhaps a forty-five minute walk." Several of those in a day could wear me out. But not them. They were energized by both the walking and the talking.

When the cold air forced us inside, we'd walk through art museums, which always generated wonderful discussions. The walls of the Hermitage are covered with gorgeous world-renowned art. My favorites were the Rembrandts. He painted so many beautiful biblical scenes that I began taking the opportunity to say to the girls, always nonchalantly, "Did you know this was in the Bible?" They, having never even so much as seen a Bible, looked stunned and then I'd tell the story. (I felt like a Vacation Bible School teacher with a flannel-graph board!)

One day, Natasha whispered to me, "I did not know so much in the Bible is about zeese paintings. Perhaps I vould vant to read zees Bible."

I've never been sure when she actually came to the realization that the Bible stories preceded the paintings. She had always thought just the opposite, but as she learned more, she began to believe the Bible might have credence.

At dinner on the last night of our first trip, Olga pulled me aside in front of the restaurant. "Madee," she whispered, not wanting to be overheard, "Debbie has told me a saying. It tis zee most beautiful saying I have ever heard. It tis 'For God so lofed the vorld that he gave his only Son to die for me.' Madee, have you ever heard this saying?"

Holding back tears, I said, "Yes. And no." While I had of course heard it all my life, I never heard it in that way. Later that night, as we walked in the cold air, postponing that inevitable parting, I said to her, "Olga, you have to know that all over the world people believe the things we've told you about the love of God. If you were to go anywhere in the world—Europe, Asia, Africa, or the Middle East—anywhere—you would find people who believe that Jesus died for us. It's not just because we are Americans. There are millions of people all over the world who believe this."

Quietly, Olga responded, "Yes. And in Leningrad, there are four who believe." She pointed to herself and her small circle of friends—Natasha, Svetlana, and Elena.

Reluctantly, we left the next morning, and shortly afterward the first of many letters arrived in my mail. It was before any of us had laptop computers; so we were dependent on pen, ink, and a very slow ineffectual postal system. I'll never forget that initial letter from Leningrad. "Dear Mary, the day you left, winter came." Even now, twenty-five years later, thinking of that makes me melancholy.

On the second trip, I met another Svetlana, and as we discussed the gospel message, she asked a question I've never forgotten. In America, in my work with university students, we often spoke of God having a plan for their lives—a destiny, if you will. That did not translate well into Russian since the communists, unfortunately, had a coercive plan for their lives. So our translators used the word "dream."

One day over tea, I said to Svetlana, "God loves you, Svetlana. He has a dream for your life."

She stopped me midsentence, and with her eyes beginning to tear, she whispered in her heavy accent, "Is this true? God has a dream about my life?"

I assured her it was true, so she leaned across the table and in the softest imaginable voice said, "Does he *know* I am a Soviet citizen?"

Isn't that what we all feel when we hear God loves us but are thinking of that one thing that might disqualify us? *Does he know?*

The reality is, God has a dream for all our lives. You, me, and yes, even a nineteen-year-old Soviet citizen who'd never heard of him, are *his* unique and wonderful creation. We were made for him. He loves us and has dreams for our lives.

When I look back, as I often do to those wonderful young women we met—and later their friends and their friends' friends—I can still hear Natasha saying, "Madee, tell them vhat you told us. Zey vant to know."

Every single time we were there, the joy was unspeakable. But when we did speak of it, it was in hushed and quiet tones. We whispered. Something about it was so unbelievable even to us as seasoned Christians that we didn't want to denigrate the joy of it into mere words.

Here were these girls, a million miles from us in their experience, lifestyle, belief system, age, and stage of life. We had nothing in common with them. We tried to bridge the gap culturally, but it was so obvious that we didn't. They wanted only one thing from us—they wanted to sound like Americans, but they couldn't because they'd never met an American (and had never even seen an American movie or TV show). But God had a far greater purpose in mind. He knew, as did we, that they were missing nothing by not sounding like an American teenager. And he also knew, as did we, that they were missing everything by not knowing him.

It amazes me that there are people all over the world just like those students—people for whom Christ died and people he plans to find a way to reach with the message of his love and forgiveness. He made us to know him and to have a relationship with him, no matter where we were born, or under what political system. He will find a way to connect his message with people.

Sometimes joy is shouted from the rooftops; sometimes it's spoken softly in tones barely audible. Some of the greatest joy I've ever known has been in clandestine places, secret meetings, subdued conversations. Those times have given me a new appreciation for Psalm 46:10, which I've heard all my life: "Be *still*, and know that I am God."

~ *O God, we worship you in shouts of joy and whispers of praise. We lay our hearts at your holy feet and bow our heads in humility in your presence. Give us courage, O Lord, to share the glorious message of your love and grace with those around us in whatever way we must so they can come to know you. In Jesus's precious name, amen.*

Too Happy to Hold Back

BARBARA JOHNSON

᠅ ✳ ᠅

Then they cried out to the LORD in their trouble, and he brought
them out of their distress. He stilled the storm to a whisper; the
waves of the sea were hushed. (PSALM 107:28–29 NIV)

My husband, Bill, was never very good at whispering. His hearing was damaged during his days as a navy pilot back in World War II, and since he couldn't hear very well, his "whispers" often came out as loud as—or sometimes even louder than—normal conversation. It caused a few embarrassing moments here and there, and I rammed my elbow into his ribs so many times to get him to quiet down that it's a wonder he didn't have a permanent dent in his side.

For instance, while we were traveling with Women of Faith, we would sometimes be assigned to a local hostess whose driving skills were, shall we say, on the exciting side. Most of the time Bill rode in the front seat, and that arrangement always worried me a little because I knew if he started "muttering" critical comments to himself I wouldn't be able to reach him with my elbow.

Occasionally, though, our hostess would have a van, and Bill and I would settle into one of the seats in the back. Then when he turned to me and "whispered" what he thought of her terrifying tailgating or her in-and-out lane changes, I could cut him off before his loud voice reached the front seat.

Bill's inability to whisper came into play most noticeably when Billy Graham's crusade came to our area several years ago. As always, hundreds of volunteers were needed to help with the event, and I signed up to sing in the choir—partly because I knew I would enjoy the experience, and partly because I knew choir members were guaranteed good seats. Then I realized Bill would want to attend the crusade as well, so I signed him up for the choir, too, even though, as they say, he couldn't carry a tune in a bucket.

During rehearsals, I encouraged Bill to just mouth the words as the choir sang or at least to just whisper them, and he did his best to do that—right up until the time the crusade actually began. Then, swept up in all the excitement and the glory of the musical worship, Bill burst forth into song along with the thousands of others in the choir and the audience.

It wouldn't have been a problem, except that he carried a little tape recorder in his shirt pocket so we could listen to the crusade program again later—and let me just say, there was *nothing* enjoyable about listening to Bill sing in that loud, booming, off-key voice of his!

Actually, that isn't quite right either. My friends and family and I *did* laugh until we cried as we listened to that tape, and Bill was a good sport, so he just laughed along with us. In fact, just thinking about it now, after all these years, still makes me chuckle. I wish I had saved it to replay now that Bill's moved on to heaven. I smile to think he's singing in the heavenly choir now, and I know his voice is as sweet as that of the other angels.

There are so many funny stories about people whose "whispers" are more like shouts. Kids are the most common culprits. I love the story about the little boy who was afraid his mother was going to sleep through Communion. As the elders moved down the aisle, bringing the trays of wafers and the tiny cups of grape juice, he shouted, "Mom, wake up! Here come the drinks!"

To be honest, most of the time I'm like that little boy—and like Bill in the midst of the choir. When something wonderful is happening, I have a hard time restraining myself from shouting with joy when a whisper might have been more appropriate.

And then there have been those *other* times . . . those dark and difficult days when even a whisper was more than I could muster: when a military car stopped in front of our house and two marines in dress uniform came to tell us our son Steven had died in Vietnam . . . When a Royal Canadian Mounted Police officer called to say our son Tim had been killed by a drunk driver in the Yukon . . .

Those were times when I could hardly breathe, let alone speak. But friends and family rushed in to help, and even though the pain was overwhelming, at least I had peace, knowing that our two sons are now my deposits in heaven.

But when we learned that a third son was a homosexual, things were different. I could barely bring myself to say the word, and the few people I confided in had no idea what I needed. I called a crisis phone line and said in a voice that could barely be heard, "I need help. I'm the mother of a h-h-h-h-homosexual."

But there was no help for mothers like me back then. Almost no one would admit to having a homosexual in their family. As one mom told me later, "My son came out of the closet—and I went in."

I told her I knew that closet well. That's where I hid, in my emotional weakness, to whisper those "groans that words cannot express," as Romans 8:26 describes them. But that's also where "the Spirit himself" interceded for me, as that verse goes on to say. Eventually I was able to come out of that dark place and extend a helping hand to other parents whose hearts had been broken and whose words had been reduced to sobs and whispers.

Bill and I started Spatula Ministries to help parents like us, parents whose adult children had died or were homosexuals or had caused their parents trouble in some other way. Over the years I've heard from thousands of those parents, mostly moms. Sometimes they call and are unable to talk at all. At first I think it's a bad connection. Then maybe I'll hear a little sob, or a small, soft voice that whispers, "Barb . . ."

And I know what's coming: a sad story of heartache and

despair, usually told in a shaky voice that's strained by tears and broken by sobs.

When I first found myself in that hard place all those years ago, I felt like an elephant was sitting on my chest, my teeth were growing fur, and a shag run was stuck in my throat. In fact, I've had those experiences again in the last few years:

When the doctor came into my hospital room following exploratory surgery and said, "I'm sorry. It's cancer" . . . When I was confined to a rehabilitation center, weakened by the effects of chemotherapy and unable to do anything for myself due to two broken arms, and learned that Bill had bone cancer . . . And, later, when he died . . .

Oh, the pain that can reduce our voices to whispers and whimpers!

But here's the good news. No matter what kind of difficult situation you find yourself in right now, there *is* a way out of it. Don't let yourself stay mired down in the cesspool. Find some help—a friend or a professional who can help you catch your breath and find your voice again. I've said it for years, but it's still true today: pain is inevitable, but *misery is optional*. Don't choose that option! There's plenty of pain out there, ready to wreck your life, but there's even more joy. Just look for it, and when you find it—share it.

Some of the most joyful people I know are men and women who've endured terrible hurts and tremendous losses. It would be perfectly understandable if they shut themselves off from the world and lived life as a sad and sorrowful whisper. Instead, they have clung to God's promise that they're bound for glory, and while they're still here on earth they seek out joy anywhere they can think to look for it. Then, when they find it, they let it fill their lives until it just has to overflow. Everywhere these people go, there is laughter—and not the quiet kind, either.

They're the ones I want to sit by the next time I'm scheduled for chemotherapy or stuck in some doctor's waiting room. While everyone else in the room may be whispering about the long wait or detailing their latest ailments, these folks are telling jokes about their hair falling out or repeating some funny comment a grandchild made about their prosthesis. They're too happy to hold back—and I want to be one of them!

Dear Jesus, your Word whispers encouragement to my soul and joy to my heart. Help me be still so that I can hear your still, small voice guiding me through difficult times and leading me to joyful days. Amen.

PART 4

Joy Celebrates

Celebration!

Patsy Clairmont

ๆ ✳ ๆ

Eye has not seen, nor ear heard . . . the things which God has pre-
pared for those who love Him. (1 Corinthians 2:9 NKJV)

W hat denotes a celebration for you? Family? Friends?
Food? Flowers? Gifts? Or all of the above? Yes, me too. And
that's just what I received for my sixtieth birthday. My darling
hubby lavished me with five dozen red and yellow roses—yes,
dozen! Count them: one for each year of my life. Yikes! It was
startling to look at this mammoth bouquet and realize I've lived
that long! But it also was breathtaking for Les to remember me
in such a romantic way.

The roses were next to a banquet table of friends who had
gathered from near and far to surprise me. And surprised I was.
We had a wonderful dinner, a yummy cake, and then I had the
delight of opening some very fun gifts. I love a joyous party!

Speaking of party, I've often wondered what it would have

been like to be an Israelite when they crossed through the Red Sea and stepped out safely on the other side. Talk about a reason to celebrate! No wonder Miriam and the women picked up timbrels and danced as Miriam sang,

> Sing to the LORD,
>> for He has triumphed gloriously!
>> The horse and its rider
>> He has thrown into the sea! (Exodus 15:21 NKJV)

Or how about when the prodigal son returned home? Remember the dad threw a party to celebrate the homecoming of his runaway son? I would have loved being on that guest list just to see the father's relieved face of joy. Reunions are so touching. Why, I get teary-eyed even watching at airports when folks are being reunited, and I don't even know them. It's all I can do to not run up and join the embrace.

Yes, there's just something about a celebration that makes one's foot start to tap and one's heart begin to boogie. Unless you are the prodigal's brother. He was the son who had followed all his father's rules, showed up for work on time, and taken care of every detail. He had been the responsible one and was in no mood to have a party for his careless brother. No one had recognized and applauded all his diligence, so why would they celebrate his little brother's insurrection?

Do you ever feel hesitant to enter into the good fortune of others because you feel they don't deserve recognition or because their party only emphasizes the pain you feel because no one has acknowledged you?

I have to admit that I see the older brother's point. If I'd done all I could to always be a contributing factor, and the gold medallion went to the gal who spent most of her time filing her fake fingernails, I wouldn't be happy either.

Of course, the father didn't throw a party because his son had been rebellious, but he was rejoicing that when his son's heart turned toward home, he had arrived with a whole new belief system. The son no longer felt entitled, self-empowered, greedy, or arrogant. No, he returned deeply repentant and truly humble. Now *repentant* and *humble*, folks, are party words, especially to a parent!

So the older brother's point fades quickly in the light of transformation, redemption, and God's truth: "My thoughts are not your thoughts, nor are your ways My ways" (Isaiah 55:8 NKJV). What we value may be something God despises.

The Pharisees often proved that. They thought all their righteous promenading would impress God and be winsome to others. Instead, the Lord instructed them to pray in a closet, wash the feet of their workers, and prefer others above themselves. God's desires couldn't have been further away from the behavior of the religious men of the day.

Yes, envy, superiority, boasting, jealousy, loathing, and the like are not good dance partners and will ultimately impede our longing for a joy-filled celebration.

The word *celebration* makes me wonder what heaven will be

like. We know there will be singing, food, family, and a Guest of Honor. No one will resent his presence or his position. All anger, strife, and self-serving will be done away with, and we'll all be grateful and honored we are on the guest list.

Have you ever tried to picture heaven? Me too. But I just can't quite *see* it. My binoculars are fogged over with the restrictions of earth.

When I celebrated my birthday, the table was long and filled with people I love. The centerpiece was crowded with gorgeous lilies, roses, and daisies. The sweet fragrance wafted throughout the room mingling with the festivities.

Gratefully, at the Lord's "party" his celebration table will be long and crowded with his people. I can't begin to imagine the flowers that will grace the table. I have a feeling they will emit more than fragrance. In fact, I wonder if they won't sing of the Host and applaud his presence. There will be species we've never seen and colors we couldn't have dreamed up. Perhaps some will be spun from cashmere, tatted from silk, or woven with gold filaments to catch his light. And the fragrances I'm sure will be sweeter than gardenias and more appealing than the aroma of morning coffee.

The dishes will cause Tiffany's offerings to look like discarded paper plates. Adorning each table setting will be plates designed out of transparent rainbows with utensils fashioned from white, billowing clouds with our new names monogrammed on them.

And food? What a menu that will be: the wine of his company, holy manna, a love-joy-peace soup, and what else for dessert but heaven's version of angel food cake complete with luminous halos.

Of course I'm being absurd because we can't, try as we might, begin to imagine how divine it will be. First Corinthians 2:9 tells us, "Eye has not seen, nor ear heard, nor have entered into the heart of man the things which God has prepared for those who love Him" (NKJV). Think of the most beautiful place you've ever been and know it pales to what awaits us.

Revelation offers us some stirring pictures of our divine future: thirst-quenching fountains (21:6), precious stones, clear as crystal (21:11), walls of jasper, gold like clear glass (21:18), gates of pearls (21:21), and trees whose leaves heal (22:2), among other things. Awesome! And that's peripheral when compared to the brilliant beauty of the Lamb of God. I have a sense that in his presence we will not want to eat but only to worship. Heaven will redefine *celebration* for us. It will definitely take it and us to new levels.

Until then we must be satisfied with balloons and confetti and a willingness in spite of difficulties to celebrate the here and now knowing one day we will be in the ever-after. So where do we begin when life can be such a downer? (Have you watched the news lately?) I believe the key to celebration is a grateful heart, which means we search daily for reasons to stand up and shout, "Let's party!"

Here's a gratitude jump-start list:

Bumping into an old friend
Making a new friend
Raindrops on petals
Songbird's aria
Quiet hour
Meaningful conversation
Resolving conflict
Butterfly's dance
A child's giggle
A yummy book
Open flowers
Shared laughter
Sweet dreams
Soft pillows
Starlit nights

Now join in and extend the list to include all the marvelous reasons *you* have to be upbeat and confetti-ready. Celebrate, girlfriend! Celebrate!

↬ *O Lord, thank you for the joy of celebration and a life that is so rich from our relationship with you that we want to celebrate all the time. We love you, Lord. We praise you, and we want to share this contagious joy with everyone we know. In Jesus's name, amen.*

Filling Your Blessing Basket

SHEILA WALSH

ᰔ ✳ ᰔ

Parents will tell their children what you have done. They will retell
your mighty acts, wonderful majesty, and glory. And I will think
about your miracles. They will tell about the amazing things you do,
and I will tell how great you are. They will remember your great
goodness and will sing about your fairness. (PSALM 145:4–7 NCV)

I was born in Scotland, went to college in London, England, and first set foot on American soil during a summer mission trip when I was twenty years old. I remember looking out of the plane window as we circled Manhattan before landing at JFK airport in New York. Tears ran down my cheeks. It was so exciting to look at a skyline that I had seen in movies as a little girl and dreamt that perhaps one day I would get to visit.

By my late twenties, America had become home. I embraced almost everything that was new to me. I finally accepted that you are supposed to have that much ice in your soda, and they weren't trying to rip me off because I had a funny accent. In Scotland, anything more than two cubes of ice is viewed with great suspicion. I welcomed the concept of a bucket of popcorn with every movie. At home, if it's a long movie you bring sandwiches!

The one thing I could not accept was pumpkin pie. After my very first Thanksgiving meal in the hotel where I was staying, I visited the dessert table and picked up what I thought was treacle tart or my very favorite, sticky toffee pudding in pie form. When I put that first, most delectable forkful in my mouth I nearly had a fit.

"What is this?" I whispered to an American friend who was eating with me.

"It's pumpkin pie," she said.

"Pumpkin as in 'look at all those pumpkins in the vegetable patch, Charlie Brown'?" I asked.

"Right, pumpkin pie; it's Thanksgiving!" she said.

"That is disgusting!" I replied. "Do they have any brussel sprout pie? Or how about some green bean pie?"

Despite my disgust with the "vegetable-in-sheep's clothing" thing, Thanksgiving has become one of my favorite days of the year. I love that it's not sullied by receiving gifts, but rather it's a time to stop and thank God for every gift he has lavished on us every day. Life is so busy and demanding that I'm grateful for a reminder to just stop . . . stop and see everything with which our Father has surrounded us.

Giving thanks does wonders for me. It refocuses me on what's really important so that, instead of dwelling on the fact that our dog just dropped one of my new pale blue suede pumps down the toilet, I can celebrate the gift of her sweet face, loving nature, and commitment to follow me wherever I go.

Marcus Aurelius, a first-century Roman emperor, wrote that the most important thing a man can choose is how he thinks. We can dwell every day on the things that are not working and let them drag us down, or we can thank God for the simple gifts of grace he gives us every day, if we have a heart to see them.

When Barry's mom's liver cancer had spread to the degree that she was receiving in-home hospice care, she told me about the many people who dropped by every day to say hi or to bring some crab soup to try to tempt her to eat. "Sometimes you don't stop to think how many good friends you have until a time like this," Eleanor said. "I wish I had told them how much I appreciated them more often when I was well."

That thought sat on my shoulder like a small bird waiting to be fed. One March evening when we were visiting Eleanor in Charleston, Barry and I went out for a drive through the beautiful countryside. Suddenly the idea occurred to me: "Here's what I'd like to do," I said. "We'll have a good photo taken of you and Christian and me and get it enlarged, then cut it into pieces."

Barry looked at me as if the strain of his mom's illness had pushed me off a mental bridge. "Like a jigsaw puzzle," I explained. "We'll send a piece of the puzzle to each of our dear friends with a letter telling them why we're grateful to them, what they add to our lives, and how God has used them to fill in the missing pieces in our hearts. Then at Christmas we'll invite them to a party at our house. We'll ask them to bring their piece and give them a gift specially chosen to highlight what they mean to us."

Barry was still looking at me as if I needed more sleep. I pressed on as we women have to when they don't get it. "At the end of the evening we'll glue all the pieces back together, a visual picture of how our friends have added to our lives and how truly grateful we are for each one of them."

"What made you think of that?" Barry asked as we drove across the river.

"Don't you think it's a good idea?" I asked him.

"Sure I do," he replied, "but what made you think of it?"

"I don't really know. Sometimes I just want to find more ways to say thank you."

"So you just thought of that?" Barry pressed.

"Yes."

"And you're feeling all right?"

"Yes!"

I smiled. "It's like what we're trying to teach Christian. We tell him it's not enough just to say 'sorry' when he does something wrong. Instead we ask him to tell us what he's sorry for. So perhaps it's not always enough to say 'thanks' either. We need to say what we're grateful for."

As I lay in bed that night after swallowing the two aspirin Barry gave me, I thought about how the same principle applies to our relationship with God. Instead of just tossing off a "Hey, thanks!" now and then as we hustle through life, why not make it a practice to thank him very specifically for his goodness to us and celebrate his love?

In her book *Basket of Blessings: 31 Days to a More Grateful*

Heart, Karen O'Connor shares her experience with just such a practice. "If you want to be content, to experience peace," a friend had told Karen, "write down your blessings—the things you're grateful for—on slips of paper and put them in a container of some kind. A small basket or box or bag will do. Soon it will be full to overflowing. From time to time look at what you wrote. No one can be discontent for long with so much to be thankful for."

In addition to filling a "blessing basket" on a daily basis, we could write a letter to God once a year, listing all that pours out of our hearts for his extravagant grace to us. Think of what a joy it would be to keep our annual letters of gratitude to read through the years or to pass on to our children. What a celebration we could have as we remind ourselves of the faithfulness of God.

Whether our thank-you moments are momentary, intentional pauses in the midst of a hectic day, thank-you notes to God for his many blessings, or lengthy discourses of his grace, cultivating an attitude of gratitude will remind us of the truth that undergirds our lives: "For the LORD is good and his love endures forever; his faithfulness continues through all generations" (Psalm 100:5 NIV).

Holidays like Thanksgiving, Christmas, and Easter can be joyful occasions, but I'm aware that they can be painful too. Perhaps you have lost a loved one, and this is this first time you will face a particular birthday or anniversary with an empty place at your table. Perhaps family times make you feel lonely, remind you of what's not true for you at this moment. I pray that you might know deep in your spirit that you belong to an eternal family; you are loved by God, enough for him to send his precious Son to the cross for you. We have so much to celebrate as daughters of the King of kings. I pray that you might find a quiet place today to stop and lift your heart up in gratitude to our Father.

And just think, in Scotland we are told to eat our vegetables before we get dessert; here in America you get to do both at the same time.

You are loved!

✂ *O Father, my heart overflows with love and gratitude for the enormous basket of blessings you have given me. I celebrate with joy my amazing privilege to give gifts to others in your name. Please bestow on me a double portion of your spirit of generosity and grace. Amen.*

Not Too Tick and Not Too Tin

MARILYN MEBERG

꒳ ✳ ꒳

And let your godly ones sing with joy. (PSALM 132:9 GW)

I went through a phase of motherhood, which to me seemed wise, nurturing, and imperative. My husband, Ken, called that period "Marilyn's stone-ground, sugarless" phase. I was convinced that the only way to ensure the health and well-being of my family was to avoid as much processed food as possible. Therefore, I made my own bread from stone-ground, whole-wheat flour available to me from Knott's Berry Farm where the old grist mill was still in daily operation. I made my own yogurt, was fanatical about fresh fruit and vegetables, and of course, sugar was unknown in my kitchen.

Now I must admit that with blackstrap molasses as the only sweetener I'd consider using, my food could be described as "bracing." But I felt enormously gratified that I was seeing to the nutritional well-being of my family, even though there was limited encouragement for my efforts.

One morning Mary, one of my neighbors, dropped by for a cup of tea (straight, no sugar). I was stunned when she told me my children were going from house to house asking if there were any available cookies they might snack on. Everyone in that little cul-de-sac knew my food philosophy and felt sorry for my children. Apparently there was an unending supply available for their sugar-deprived little bodies. Mary told me that Jeff was especially partial to Mystic Mint cookies, so she made sure she always had them in her pantry.

In those days no one had heard of an "intervention" for those who would benefit from such a truth encounter, but in essence that was Mary's purpose in dropping by for tea. I needed a touch of truth. At first I felt slightly betrayed by my neighbors, but as I thought more about it, I wondered if my food philosophy was a little out of balance with the world around me. It was certainly out of balance with my neighbors.

As I was discussing it all with Ken that evening (the intervention day), he said there were times when he wondered if a loaf of nutrition-laden bread might not make a better "doorstop" than breakfast food. I began to giggle over that image. I asked him why he had never said anything to me. He said, "Because your heart was so right and your intentions so pure, I didn't want to say anything. Besides I figured the kids would mutiny sooner or later anyway, and then we could talk."

We had a little family council and discussed why Mom was so

committed to her nutrition program, but I assured everyone I could compromise some. I agreed to Mystic Mints in the pantry (no more than two a day), and we had a little funeral service for the remaining blackstrap molasses. I continued to make my stone-ground, whole-wheat bread, eliminating not only the molasses but the Brewers Yeast, which lightened it up and made it much tastier. My family congratulated me; the bread-doorstop was eliminated.

Ken grew up in a Norwegian-dominated section of Seattle (Ballard). Mrs. Walvick, who lived nextdoor to his family, was a colorful little lady with predictable patterns and inflexible food habits. Every Saturday morning she went to her special Norwegian bakery, where she bought bread, rolls, and cold cuts for Saturday night sandwiches. Every Saturday morning she'd lean into the butcher's ear for the usual instruction regarding the slicing of her cold cuts. "Not too tick and not too tin," she'd say, stepping back then—confident the butcher knew exactly what she expected from his slicer.

On the night of our family chat challenging me to lighten up on my nutritional program, I told Ken that Mrs. Walvick was serving as an inspiration for me. The "not too tick and not too tin" instruction to the butcher could serve me well. Mrs. Walvick wanted balance for her cold cuts. That was achieved by not going too far in either direction. A touch of Norwegian wisdom warmly inspired me to check my own "tick or tin." Now before we close the subject of my health-food inclinations, I will say simply I still prefer stone-ground, whole-wheat bread, as well as fruits and vegetables.

When we consider the life of Jesus and the example he left us, would you say he was careful about "not too tick and not too tin"? Do you think he was balanced? You will remember he sometimes moved away from the clambering needs of the crowd. That meant many needs went unmet.

Mark 4:1 reads, "And again He began to teach by the sea. And a great multitude was gathered to Him, so that He got into a boat and sat in it on the sea; and the whole multitude was on the land facing the sea" (NKJV).

Jesus was not totally leaving the crowd to their unmet needs, but because he got into the boat to preserve his physical well-being, many were not healed by his touch, though they were strengthened by his words. Many of the people who flocked around Jesus were mostly interested in their physical healing; the teaching of Jesus may have been secondary. I interpret this incident as a balanced response by Jesus. Because of space limitations, Jesus did the best thing under the circumstances.

I've know many persons in Christian leadership who burned out because they wanted to meet every need of the people to whom they ministered, so they sacrificed themselves in the process. They didn't take care of their own health needs, emotional needs, or relational needs. It would never have occurred to them to "get in the boat" nor would they have wondered if life was "too tick or too tin."

Many years ago, I was speaking at a large event that was meant to be an evangelistic outreach to the community. It was totally spectacular: outstanding musical talent and food. I had a great time participating in this flawlessly organized evening. But the event leader was a mess. For weeks, she fussed over the details of this project. She had sacrificed her husband, her children, and her own sleep to accomplish her goal. What was her goal? That the church present to the community the claims of Christ in the most winsome way possible. In my opinion her goal was accomplished.

As her husband drove me to the airport, I commented on the flawless success of the evening. I suggested it would probably now be a relief to get his wife back. After a short silence he said, "My wife eats, sleeps, and lives for the many church events she organizes. We won't see her any more now that this is over. There's always the next crucial activity that will take all her time."

I fell silent, thinking I'd better not get into this one, but I must admit my heart hurt. It is easy to become so focused on the benefit of organization, making Christ known, knowing our lives are being lived out for a higher purpose than our own humanity, that we lose sight of balanced ministry. God had gifted this woman with a husband and children. She was laying those gifts aside that she might stay amid the throngs who needed her and wanted her. She needed to incorporate Mrs. Walvick's cold-cut philosophy—not too tick and not too tin. It would translate into greater joy in her own soul as she relaxed with Jesus in the boat.

As a young mother inordinately focused on the nutritional needs of my family, I, too, needed to get in the boat. I was out of balance. The result of being out of balance about anything is a diminished joy. I quickly learned that Mystic Mint cookies made my afternoon tea time a full-on joy celebration. I love Psalm 132:9, which says, "And let your godly ones sing with joy" (GW). We can do that with our mouths full, if we want.

↝   *Father God, please give me the wisdom to create balance in my life and the life of my family. I know I need to get in the boat and push back from the shore a little more often. Help me to find rest and peace in the boat with you. Amen.*

God Is in Control

MARY GRAHAM

༈ ✻ ༈

Cast all your anxiety on him because he cares for you.
(1 PETER 5:7 NIV)

*E*normous problems don't upset me. I take on challenges as if mountains were easily scaled. When an opportunity comes, I typically bite off more than I can chew. When I see the unthinkable, it makes me want to trust God and believe him for a miracle. Little things, however . . .

Some time ago, I was babysitting Christian Walsh's pets. His family was on a trip to Scotland; so I volunteered to keep the family menagerie, which at the time was only Belle, the dog, and Hamtaro, the hamster. I don't really understand anything at all about hamsters, but I'm crazy about Christian and would do anything he asked, including spending Christmas with a rodent.

It couldn't have been easier, until on the ninth day, early in the morning, I saw no sign of life in the hamster cage and realized

I'd seen nothing the day before either. For one dizzy moment, I thought, *Maybe the little fellow's been asleep for a couple of days.* I ran to the nearest computer and Googled the question: "Do hamsters hibernate?"

Immediately, the response came, "Only in the wild."

Shoot! So I phoned my friend Cindy, who knows everything about dogs, thinking perhaps her dog knowledge could apply to all animals. I left her a message. Then I remembered a friend whose son who had received two hamsters as a gift. After her son bonded to them, they discovered they had one male and one female, which accidentally resulted in a family of twenty hamsters in their household. So I left a message on her cell phone—surely she'd know what to do.

I decided if Hamtaro was dead in the cage, I'd take the whole thing—cage and critter—to the pet shop from which it came and ask them to do an autopsy. I wanted to ensure that he would have died anyway, even if he'd been in Christian's care.

I obsessed on this for several hours until my brave little friend, Patsy Clairmont (who happened to be staying with me at the time), awakened. Although Patsy shares freely about the huge part fear played in her life as a young girl, in this instance she was the picture of strength and exactly what I needed. She courageously opened the cage and found not a *dead* hamster but *no* hamster at all.

"Honey," she said softly, "there's no hamster in this cage."

As the mother of two sons, Patsy understood the hamster species; so she started crawling around on the floor looking in nooks and crannies. I did nothing but wring my hands. And then it hit me: we had two dogs in the house! Mine and Belle. That's it—Hamtaro's history! I knew we could really be facing a disaster here, and Christian was due home in less than twenty-four hours.

Finally, Patsy spotted a very frightened little Hamtaro under the washing machine and delivered him safely back into his cage. All was well. We celebrated with great joy!

It was then I remembered that *all* the promises of God are true, *all* the time. He can *always* be trusted. He's *always* there. He doesn't judge our requests, feelings, needs, fears, desires, inadequacies, insecurities, or vulnerabilities. He doesn't leave us on our own when our issues are too minor or too impossible to manage. He doesn't say, "I don't do hamsters."

Instead, he takes care to call us his children, his beloved, his friends. He says to us, "Come to me." I've never seen a verse, passage, or intonation in his Word that says, "Go away. Come back when you have a real need or when I have more time."

He understands we are weak and our dependence on him is constant. Whether you're frightfully aware of your need today because it's enormous (or feels that way), remember this: "Cast *all* your anxiety on him because he *cares* for *you*" (1 Peter 5:7 NIV; emphasis added).

However, having said that, I often need a reminder that he doesn't always meet our need in our timing or in our way. As difficult as it is to admit, my faith often finds its greatest reassurance in the resolution of my need in just the way I've imagined it would be resolved—happily ever after—my favorite way to end the stories of my life. I want God to do what I want him to, and when, and more often than not, even how. When I need him to find a hamster, I need him to do it *now*, and I need it *alive*.

The better I know him and his ways, though, the more I realize that is not his promise to me. His promise is this: "Many sorrows shall be to the wicked; but he who trusts in the LORD, mercy shall surround him. Be glad in the LORD and rejoice, you righteous; and shout for joy, all you upright in heart!" (Psalm 32:10–11 NKJV).

Fortunately, mercy surrounds the one who trusts the Lord, and not in her own solution. Trusting in the Lord is letting my weight fall fully on his strength, knowing he will always know what to do, and his will and way are better than my own.

As I look back over my life and my relationship with God, I realize that more often than not, I don't get my way. And, if I do, it's certainly not in my preferred time frame. I rarely get perfect results within two hours of my prayer as I did in the case of Hamtaro.

I learned this the hard way. Nearly twenty-five years ago, I lost my mother after a ten-year battle with Alzheimer's disease. She was a wonderful, capable, amazing woman. As the mother of eight children, she was, by anyone's standard, a wonder. She cared for us, managed our household, presided over the PTA, and was a faithful friend and a woman of faith. My father was often out of work. Not wanting to leave her children, Mom wrote a column for two area newspapers, making seventeen dollars a week from home and, interestingly, it never crossed my mind that we were poor. My dad was a bit of a hotheaded reactionary, but my mother was calm, cool, and collected. She held us together like glue, and we all grew up completely devoted to her.

When she began to lose track of words, ideas, and time, we responded playfully, teasing her as though she'd snap out of it. Frankly, she'd always snapped out of everything else that might have been unsettling. But not this time. Her mental health seemed to be evaporating over time; emotionally, she wasn't quite there; and physically, she wasn't the same. We were scared, but by then, except for Daddy, we'd all followed my mother into that same sustaining faith she'd demonstrated for years. So, as a family, we prayed. We begged God to make her well.

Mom was only sixty, about my age now, when the disease started stealing her from us. At the time, I'd never even heard of Alzheimer's disease. I remember when the doctor gave us the diagnosis, I said, "So. What do you do for that? Will she take medication or have surgery?" To this day I remember the look on his face. He knew, and I understood soon enough, nothing could be done. My mother had a devastating, debilitating, degenerating disease. There was no stopping it. Only death could kill it, and that was a tortuous ten-year process.

I prayed for her to get better, to feel comfortable and peaceful. She never did. I prayed we'd know what to do for her. We didn't. I wondered if I should leave my ministry, which was my full-time employment. (I was the only single sibling and the only one without children to support. Someone in my family even said to me, "Isn't it more of a ministry to take care of your own mother than to minister to strangers? It's not like you have a *real* job.") It was confusing, heartbreaking, and overwhelming.

God didn't do what we asked, but now we know he did something much better. Second Corinthians 4:16 says, "Therefore we do not lose heart. Even though our outward man is perishing, yet the inward man is being renewed day by day" (NKJV). In many ways, the weaker my mother became, the more her sweet spirit impacted our lives. As a result, we were all changed, especially my father who, after years of resistance to grace, came to personal faith in Christ. Six weeks after my mother died, he died. By then, we knew eternal life was his.

No one knows how God works. He may decide to save a hamster and wait on the suffering of one of his own children. Sometimes he chooses to allow earthly suffering for his eternal purpose. All I know is he can be trusted, even when I don't see the result. I have no need to worry, fret, or beg. He is in control, and he will accomplish his purpose. That is a joy I celebrate.

꒰ *Heavenly Father, losing someone we love is so painful. Teach us to trust you when we are emotionally vulnerable and weakened by sadness. I'm so glad that when my mother was dying, I knew that my Father was there to hold me up and lend me his strength. I love you, Father. Amen.*

Celebrating Wonder
NICOLE JOHNSON
ఌ ❋ ఌ

*Once more will I astound these people
with wonder upon wonder.* (ISAIAH 29:14 NIV)

*O*f the Seven Ancient Wonders of the World, only one remains. The Great Pyramid at Giza is the last of the aptly named ancient wonders in our modern world. For some reason, despite the urging of poets, writers, and historians to name replacements for the fallen monuments, no list can be agreed upon. So we enter our second millennium with just one ancient wonder, and this speaks volumes about what our culture thinks.

Were they all still around, I'm not sure we would appreciate the Seven Wonders of the World anymore. We would probably categorize them as the Seven Explainable Tourist Attractions. We would visit them for an hour and photograph their images with the postage-stamp-size camera on our cell phones, thinking we've really *seen* them. I've often wondered if our current ability

121

to *capture* things so quickly in this way robs us of the glory of being captured by anything. We don't have to take anything in with our memories and our hearts when we can photograph them and put them in a drawer for whenever we might want them.

As I look around, it appears that no one really does *wonder* anymore. These days we're far more into *attractions*. There is no denying that much of the building and creating going on in our country is intended for sheer amusement. I can imagine if the Great Pyramid added a water slide, people would be slipping down the sphinx before you could say Tutankhamen. In fact, I'm surprised no one has thought of it before now. Hopefully those people are not reading this devotional . . . or hopefully they *are*.

We definitely have a love affair with all things electronic. I'm a gadget girl, too, and certainly not antitechnology, but we are paying a higher price than the one on the sticker for our latest tech tools. They have easily replaced our feelings with facts and our ability to giggle with our opportunity to Google. It's the information, not the admiration, that we seem to be after.

Perhaps our culture has simply moved past *wonder*. We're over it. With the onset of globalization, there is less we've never seen and more we've seen too much. Very little takes our breath away, or silences us in sheer awe, or brings us to our knees in humble gratitude for the grandeur we see, if we even see it. There are many closed hearts that are not open to be surprised or delighted. The spirit of the age is "Been there, done that, bought the T-shirt."

Cynicism is a killer of wonder. Rarely recognizable as dangerous, cynicism grows around a heart as ivy grows around a tree. It quietly creeps, growing rapidly and choking the life from the tree, or more personally, the joy from the human heart, smothering every square inch with its *reality*. Cynicism blocks the sunlight of the sacred, stealing valuable innocence until the heart is dried up and no longer even capable of wonder or joy.

Perfectionism also kills wonder. To those of us who struggle to get things right, wonder and joy are stolen from an activity by turning it into a series of tasks. In an effort to see the Grand Canyon, many families find themselves paralyzed by the feeling of having to see it all and do it all, never looking up from their maps or their *get-'er-done* mentality. We can diminish the potential for anything to capture our hearts by focusing on what we're wearing, or in what order we're going to do things, or when our itinerary says we have to be back on the bus. We move so quickly on to the next thing in an effort and attempt to do it perfectly that we come away with very little.

Consumerism can kill wonder as well. We've become a culture of purchasers. We don't borrow sugar, or check out books, or even rent movies anymore; we *own* everything. If we borrow, or rent, or just have the chance to see something, then our hearts must do some of the work. We value the pieces we see in museums so much more because we cannot fully possess them.

Sometimes a trip to the mall is an assault on wonder. My heart gets worn down with endless possibilities of things to purchase. After I've looked at eight hundred handbags or bought a couple of pairs of shoes, my heart can be pretty calloused. The fun of shopping or even browsing can easily be replaced by the quest for better and nicer goods. I want to be seen as a woman who is up on the latest and greatest trends, but there is no wonder or awe in this; it's just a *race to the bag* literally, in order to score a point in a ridiculous game.

Wonder is not a possession to be acquired, nor can it be bought; it is merely a response, like joy. We can't make ourselves feel wonder or amazed admiration any more than we can make ourselves feel happy or hungry when we're not. We're either captured by something's greatness, or we move on quickly. But how often do we give ourselves the chance to be captured? Our pace is fast and our souls are slow. We've grown sluggish in our spirits, and our hearts have closed to wonder. Rarely do our jaws drop in amazed admiration; they're too busy yawning or criticizing.

What else can possibly explain the restless boredom that often plagues our children, or adults for that matter? We are surrounded by more options for *play* than any other generation in history. Many children act like bored middle-aged people. And many adults behave like bored children. I observe teenagers and adults alike who believe they've seen the world, and yet their hearts have been captured by nothing.

History may very well call this the Las Vegas generation of stimulation, who are, as another author put it, amusing ourselves to death. I was disheartened recently, when on a trip to Florence, Italy, I saw an anxious father scouring a map trying to find a place for lunch. I overheard him promise his teenage charges, "I know there is a Hard Rock Café around here somewhere."

Now don't be fooled into thinking that I don't like the Hard Rock Café; I have no problem with eating a burger and fries, but in Florence, Italy? Another vote for the *known and safe* against the *risk of something foreign*. How will this family ever find wonder if they only stay close to what they know? They will find lunch, but they won't find what they might really be hungry for, any more than slipping down the slide of the Sphinx would ever satisfy the yearning to unlock a mystery of the ages.

Wonder is so critical to the good life and a healthy heart. We need more than one ancient wonder in our world and in our hearts. We need to surround ourselves by things that humble us by their complexity, as opposed to things that we can purchase that bore us by their accessibility. Can we seek to take in more of the world around us than Disneyland or the Hard Rock Café? What might we do differently to cultivate real beauty into our lives on a daily basis, and how might we slow down enough to enjoy it?

This call to embrace wonder is not about what food you eat or avoiding Las Vegas; it's about sharing a perspective that calls us to celebrate real life as opposed to clutching its predictable, common trappings. It's about avoiding cynicism in our hearts, or perfectionism in our activities, or consumerism in our purchases—all of which lead to boredom and the death of wonder.

We not only have the opportunity, but we also have a responsibility to God who created the world to regain our ability to marvel and wonder at its goodness, lest we become spoiled, ungrateful children. Wonder isn't something that we can only experience on a vacation to a deserted island or when we are standing in front of a magnificent piece of art; it's what happens when we take our hearts off their leashes and let them run free. We can do that on the freeway in the middle of a traffic jam or as we watch a child pick up his toys in his bedroom. Because the wonder doesn't live in the vacation or even in the toys on the floor; it lives inside our unencumbered human hearts.

↬ *O God of wonder, I am overwhelmed at the very thought of your omnipotence and shimmering glory. To know that I'm a child of the Almighty King of heaven overflows my heart with joy! Help me, O Lord, to never lose the wonder of knowing you. Amen.*

PART 5

❧

Joy Laughs

Tea Time and Supper

MARILYN MEBERG

∿ ✳ ∿

Laughter and bread go together.
(ECCLESIASTES 10:19 MSG)

I had said, "Never in a million years will I move from Palm Desert, California, to Frisco, Texas." With typical regional arrogance, I believed California to be the only place on earth worthy of loyalty and affection.

So why did I sell my condo in Palm Desert and buy a house in Frisco? Well, here's what seems to have happened. My friend Ney Bailey was driving me around Frisco one morning in search of a good spot for a photo-shoot the next day. The photographer wanted an outdoor scene with trees. I've lived in an apartment in Frisco for a few months each year simply because flying from Dallas during our heavy travel season is easier than flying out of Palm Springs, but in those years I didn't ever remember seeing trees. For that matter, I had not seen any hills either, but we apparently didn't need a hill. Ney knew where there were some trees.

We settled on the spot for the photo-shoot, but as we were driving away, I saw a house. It beckoned to me. It didn't have any trees, but it was on a lake. The lake is lovely and only a stone's throw from Luci Swindoll's new house. It's four doors down from Nicole Johnson, a three-minute walk from Mary Graham, and a five-minute drive from Sheila and Barry Walsh. I bought the house and moved into treeless Frisco on December 18, 2004. Mercy!

What a wonder all this is. What draws me to do what I said I'd never do is not only God's relentless pushing and pulling, but my love of community. My community is fast congregating in Frisco. God seems to think I need to be there. I like that about him. I didn't put that plan into motion; he did.

Why is community so important to me? I'm sure it's because I'm an only child. I am energized by the presence of people. Growing up in somewhat isolated and rural communities, I didn't always find a sufficient number of people around. Thank goodness for Mrs. Dunbar.

Mrs. Dunbar was a short bike's ride from my house in Amboy, Washington. We had a weekly tea time at three o'clock each Tuesday. I loved visiting with her because she made the best cookies I've tasted in my short two hundred and six years on this earth. Each Tuesday she made a different cookie for our tea times. When I'd walked into her old rambling house across the street from Wires Cleaners, I'd nearly faint from the glorious smell of just-out-of-the-oven cookies. But not only did I love her cookies, one of her favorite activities in life was to laugh. We made a great pair because its one of my favorite activities as well.

Mrs. Dunbar had an ill-fitting pair of false teeth that clicked when she talked. She would put me in hysterics by sliding the bottom teeth out of her mouth as far as she could. The goal was to keep them from falling to the floor before she managed to lift them high enough to touch the end of her nose. When she succeeded, we rewarded ourselves with another cookie. By the way, it was considered cheating to use her hands to help the teeth touch the end of her nose.

I was devastated when Mrs. Dunbar died suddenly of an apparent heart attack. Her son told my father how peaceful she looked lying in bed when he found her. Everything was in order: glasses on top of her Bible, aspirin bottle on the night stand beside her teeth in a glass. I knew it would sound weird if I asked permission to have her teeth, so I kept my mouth shut. But the memory of her laughter and the sight of her teeth meant the world to me. I'd love to live in a community full of Mrs. Dunbars.

The Russian writer Aleksandr Solzhenitsyn said, "It is not the level of prosperity that makes for happiness but the kinship of heart to heart and the way we look at the world that knits us together." Those are my requirements for a successful community. Amy Cella, Nicole Johnson's assistant, is also in this community. She not only meets the requirements, but she, too, is only minutes away from the rest of us. There is a special kinship of heart between us.

Last Sunday some of the community had brunch together after church. I turned to Amy and asked, "What's the best thing that happened to you this week?"

Without the slightest hesitation she said, "I bought a cow."

That was one of those delicious fork-dropping moments.

"You what?" nearly everyone chorused. I was envisioning PetSmart and wondering how such a purchase could be made.

Sheila, who was absolutely incredulous, said, "Why? Why would you want to buy a cow?"

I was still lost in PetSmart.

"I bought the cow for food," Amy said.

Still unable to fathom this action, Sheila said, "Are you that sick of grocery shopping? You know our new Kroger is a nice store—it's only two minutes from your house."

"No, that's not the problem," Amy persisted. "I just want to raise my own beef. I'll feed it only the best 'cow food' and be sure it gets superior care."

Patsy warned Amy about getting attached to the cow. Sheila suggested not giving the cow a name to restrict possible bonding.

"Oh, I've already named the cow," Amy said. "I'm going to call it Supper." Then after it's grown I can invite people for Supper."

I did one of my spontaneous and obnoxious hoot laughs; there was no getting me under control, in spite of the many disapproving looks I got. That laugh was as hearty as those inspired by Mrs. Dunbar's touch-the-nose-with-the-bottom-teeth trick.

Actually, as I thought about it, I fully understood what Amy is doing. She is raising her recently purchased Supper on a ranch about fifteen minutes from here. We used to do the same thing in the Amboy days. Dad would buy a beef cow, raise it on Harry Hooper's farm, and then off to slaughter it went. We would then stop by Boehm's Deep Freeze every few days and bring home supper. I remember hating it, though. I had named one of the suppers Molly and felt tremendously disloyal as I looked at her on my plate.

Recently I read a newspaper account of a ninety-one-year-old woman who was enthusiastically joining neighborhood friends for a slumber party. The party was from 7 p.m. to 10 p.m. They came in robes, pajamas, and slippers and left whenever they got tired. I can see that happening some thirty years from now in Frisco. I love the notion of being with my dear community right up until the time of slumber parties.

It was Plato who said, "Let me tell you, the more the pleasures of the body fade away, the greater to me is the pleasure and charm of conversation." The only pleasure Plato failed to mention that so characterizes my community is laughter. We will always have conversation . . . we will always have laughter. What a joy!

    Lord, give us laughter, because it saves us from the sadness of facing daily life and the end of life. Lord, give us joy! Amen.

Look for the Laugh

BARBARA JOHNSON

৵ ✲ ৵

God will let you laugh again;
you'll raise the roof with shouts of joy. (JOB 8:21 MSG)

$\mathcal{M}$ y friend Lynda loves to laugh more than just about anyone I know. She's 100 percent sanguine—full of joy, quick to laugh, and completely disorganized. That last characteristic tends to make Lynda a master at living amid the chaos caused by such things as lost phone numbers, forgotten names, and assorted machines and appliances she has no idea how to work. Such problems might drive other people crazy, but Lynda joyfully accepts these challenges as a normal part of life.

It's not unusual for her to call me, asking if I remember the name of her doctor and when her next appointment is. To be honest, I'm not that much better than she is at remembering such details, and with all the doctors and appointments I've had in the last few years since my cancer diagnosis, our conversations often go something like this:

"Barb, didn't I tell you I have a doctor's appointment sometime next week?"

"I seem to remember you said something about making one."

"Well, was it the doctor whose name starts with an R or a W? I can't remember."

"I thought you said you would be sure to remember this time because this is the doctor that reminds you of a vegetable . . . or was he the one with the same name as an Old Testament prophet . . . ?"

"Hmm. I was thinking it was the doctor I see for my stomach trouble . . . or is this my appointment with the chiropractor?"

"Lynda, you really should write down these appointments!"

"Oh, Barb, I did write it down. But I lost the paper."

Life is always interesting when Lynda's around, because every day she loses something new—and while she's looking for it, she usually finds something old that she lost a month or a year ago. Every discovery prompts a gleeful celebration and another excited phone call to share her joy with me.

Lynda makes friends wherever she goes and always has a good story to tell about how that person helped, entertained, or inspired her, whether it's a street person who hangs out near the bookstore where she works or someone she meets in the doctor's waiting room.

Things haven't been easy for Lynda. She's endured heartbreaking loss and bottomless grief. But the thing about Lynda is, for all the things she loses in her everyday life, she can find the funny factor in any calamity. You can count on it. And Lynda's sister Terri has the same humor-hunting gift.

For instance, when Lynda and Terri were keeping vigil at their sweet mother's deathbed and they realized their mother was slipping away, Lynda leaned down and whispered, "Remember, Mommy, we'll meet at the eastern gate."

She was referring to a favorite gospel song about heaven that she and her mother loved to sing together. But at that time Terri had been living far away and didn't get to spend as much time with her mother as Lynda did, so she wasn't up to date on her mother's favorite hymns.

"What?" Terri exclaimed. "No one told me about meeting at the eastern gate. Who decided it would be the *eastern* gate? If nobody'd told me, I'd probably be waiting at the *western* gate, asking Jesus, 'Where *is* everybody?'"

Even as their hearts were breaking, the sisters laughed.

More recently, Terri asked Lynda if she could borrow the videotape of their parents' fiftieth anniversary party, which had been held many years earlier. Terri wanted to show her husband all the friends and relatives they hadn't seen for many years. Several of the people on the tape had died since the anniversary, and Terri wanted to see them again. Plus, she thought it would be fun for her and her husband to see their kids when they were little. Of course Lynda obliged. Then, a few days later, came the dreaded phone call.

"Oh, Lynda, something awful has happened."

"What, Terri? Are you OK?" Lynda asked.

"Oh, Lynda, it's so awful I can't stand it. It's terrible. It's horrible. It's . . ."

"Terri, is everyone all right? Has anyone died?"

"Lynda, you know Mom and Dad's anniversary tape? Well . . . I taped over it."

"Terri, how *could* you!" Lynda shrieked. "That's the only copy! Oh, I can't believe you did that."

Both sisters were crying, and then Lynda remembered something she had heard a comedian say not too long ago: "If all you've got is pain, then all you've got is pain. But if you can *laugh,* then you can *use* the pain to make your life better."

Choking back sobs, Lynda said, "Terri, stop crying. We have to think of something to laugh at, or this whole thing will just be pain. Think of something, Terri—quick."

Terri paused and then said, "Well, Lynda, you know how I've always wanted you to watch that show *Reba*? Well, now you can."

And then they laughed. And as they laughed they thought of reasons why the tape wasn't all that important anyway: most of the people on the tape were old people, and their kids wouldn't know who the old people were, and the like.

"We have our memories, and that's better than any old videotape anyway," Lynda said.

"Yes, but you know, your memory's been slipping lately."

"Oh, who cares?" Lynda replied. "It's not like we'll never see those people again—we'll see most of them in heaven."

For nearly twenty years, Lynda has been my close friend and devoted encourager. What a blessing she has been to me, always bringing with her the gift of laughter whenever she calls or visits.

One day she brought a magazine clipping that described a weight-control plan she thought would make me laugh. According to this method, doctors have you swallow a balloon that is then inflated inside your stomach to make you feel full so you don't want to eat.

The thing that made us laugh was the balloon's removal system. It had a string attached to it that would snake back up your esophagus and hang out your nose! Lynda and I had the best time brainstorming about how it would be to have that string hanging out our noses—and all the answers we could give to explain what it was to the people who asked: "Oh this? I just pull it to turn on the light in my brain. You know, whenever I want to have a light-bulb moment." Or we could tie a bead to the end of the string and make a fashion statement, or we could just stuff the string back up into our nostrils so it was out of sight, at least until we sneezed.

Lynda and I have shared a lot of laughs over the years, and that laughter has been a lifeline that has saved me from the cesspool of misery many times. It's also provided fodder for some of my writing, including the time I called her and said, "Oh, Lynda, I hope you won't be mad at me. I wrote about your bra in my new book." (She'd shown up at my house one day looking especially sharp, and when I commented on how good she looked she confessed she was wearing a new bra called Nobody's Perfect. That just *had* to go into one of my books!)

In addition to laughter, Lynda and I have also shared a strong, unwavering faith in God, who gives us both tears and laughter. Despite the challenges we've faced, we've come out on the other side with the same attitude as the Old Testament character Hannah. She was tormented for years by her childlessness, and when the Lord answered her plea for a child, Hannah prayed, "The LORD has filled my heart with joy. . . . I can laugh at my enemies; I am glad because you have helped me!" (1 Samuel 2:1 NCV).

For Hannah, the enemies were her barrenness and the women who scoffed at her because of it. For me, the enemies have been such things as grief and loss, cancer and diabetes. But despite those hardships, God has given me laughter-loving friends like Lynda, and he has "filled my heart with joy."

He'll do the same for you. Ask him to help you find the laughter in the painful problems you face. Ask him to send you a friend whose heart is so full of joy it splashes over onto you. Laugh with her at every opportunity, and if the opportunity doesn't readily present itself . . . hunt it down!

And then *be* that kind of friend to someone else.

᠕ *God of comfort, Lord of laughter, thank you for friends who help me laugh in spite of hardships. Please help me be that kind of laughter-loving friend myself. Amen.*

An Attitude of Gratitude Produces Praise, Joy, and Laughter

THELMA WELLS

ϡ ✻ ϡ

I will bless the LORD at all times;
His praise shall continually be in my mouth. (PSALM 34:1 NKJV)

*I*n the midst of terrorists' threats, no known cure for AIDS, crime, poverty, economic slowdown, religious unrest, moral decay, and more, I awoke a few days ago to the beauty of the Florida sun. When I looked up into the billowing, soft, cottony clouds embraced by the clear sky that hovered over the ground of thick, green trees and towering palm trees, a surge of gratitude swelled in my chest.

I began to thank God for the sky and the earth. I was grateful for the cars and buses racing down the striped freeway and marveled at how those white lines help keep people from crashing into each other.

There were signs guiding the way to different destinations

and signal lights that ensure safety. An airplane glided through the air easily. White housetops glistened as they stood at attention while businesses laced their circumference.

There in the middle of it all, floating in the breeze, was the flag of the United States of America.

I'm so glad to be an American!

Just as the calm waters flowed softly in the tributary below my hotel window, I heard the sweet voice of Jesus laughing softly in my heart, "I did it all for you."

When I think of the graciousness and goodness of the Lord and everything he has done for us, my soul and spirit shouts, "Hallelujah!" Hallelujah is the highest praise to God. And one of my favorite things to do is to offer praises to him who deserves all our praise.

If you were to make a list of all the things you are thankful for, what would they be? Would they be health, strength, stamina, hope, happiness, or a heart of love? Would they include peace, prosperity, position, poise, and power? Could you add intelligence, initiative, and intuition? What about listening, learning, and laughter?

Can you praise him for commitment, concern, competence, and a contagious personality? Given the time and space in this devotional, I could add about a hundred thousand things for which to be grateful. But if you're like me, I get bored with lists.

On my list, however, I would include people, books, references, Internet, e-mail, coworkers, family, friends, and enemies (they encourage me to pray). And I can't forget my bags of pantyhose with the runs in them that I wear under my trousers (they are soooo necessary).

If we each had a legal pad, we couldn't even remember all the things we have for which to be thankful. If we had the full 168 hours in a week to speak and sing praises to God for what he has done for us, we wouldn't be able to complete them, because as soon as we finish praising him for one thing, he gives us something else.

Now, that's just like God.

We sing a song in our church that says, "You can't beat God giving, no matter how you try." That's so true. I've even tried to imagine giving God everything—all of me—and I surmised that it wouldn't come close to what he has done for me.

A lot of these blessings are so obvious that we tend to take them for granted, like breathing. I just do it. I take for granted that I can move my limbs and blink my eyes. I just do it. I take no thought of my ability to walk. I just do it. It's a startling thought when we realize that some people can't "just do it."

One of the most grateful, praise-giving people I can remember was named Dorothy Nell Calhoun. From birth until she died, she couldn't just do it. Her entire right side was paralyzed from her arm that was in a bent-elbow position, to her fingers that were stacked on top of each other with no flexibility to open. Her leg was in a semicircle twist inward, and her foot was turned with her toes facing her other leg. Not a pretty sight to onlookers. However, every day of her life when she could stand on those legs and brace herself with her good arm and hand, she was determined to make the best out of her paralyzed situation.

At eighteen years of age, she was forced to live on her own and make it with her little baby girl. She lived in servants' quarters in her hometown where she was employed as a maid washing clothes and cleaning someone else's house. Her life was haunted with jobs that paid very little.

With one good arm, one good leg, and one good foot, she stood all day pressing clothes in a laundry without scorching the people's clothes. She clipped tags at a clothing store without cutting herself. She sorted clothes for a national charitable organization. In all of this, I noticed her gratitude for having a job and saw her praising God for what we "just do" that she could not do.

From a comfortable and warm home with her parents, to the servants' quarters, to the tent without floors, to the high-rise apartment for the disabled, to the rehabilitation center, she demonstrated an overwhelming gratitude to God for all he had done for her and continually praised God for his gifts of kindness to her, even in her condition.

I'm an eyewitness to this human, heartfelt praiser, because Dorothy Nell Calhoun was my mother. I remember her wanting to be successful so much that she entered barber college, graduated, but was unable to get a job in a barber shop because people didn't want someone with a crippled hand working on their head with a razor. Do you think that stopped her? Absolutely not! She would go up and down the apartments cutting the residents' hair. When she didn't go to them, they would come to her. Hallelujah! Nothing could stop her except poor health that rendered her bedridden.

Do you think that's where I learned to laugh and praise? My sister is a praiser. My children love to laugh and praise God. Even my grandchildren sing, shout, and play in praise. It seems to be a family affair. Sometimes it's just not expedient to yell out praise to God in the grocery store or a fine boutique, but inwardly I'm in a state of gratitude and praise all the time. I often catch myself chuckling or moving my head.

My soul cries out silently within me, *Thank you, Lord! You are so good to me! You've given me peace in the time of war and destruction. You've given me beauty in a world of cruelty. You've given me hope in the middle of despair. How I appreciate you!*

Sweet ladies, when you find yourselves saddened by the world's vices, just say with me, "Thank you, Lord, for surrounding me with your beauty and protection. I really appreciate all you're doing for me!" When you look around and see all the things he's given you, just say, "Praise you, Lord!" When you attempt to list everything he's done for you, don't forget to list the things we take for granted and the things we *just do*.

When people are down and out, feeling sorry for themselves, empathize with them (without lofty platitudes), sharing that even in the midst of trouble we can be grateful that God is helping us go through our problems. We can thank him because he never leaves us or forsakes us. We can follow his dictates to praise the Lord in the good times, the bad times, and between times because he blesses us all the time.

In Nehemiah 8:10, people were down and out, crying and hurting because of something for which they were not even responsible. Nehemiah lifted their spirits by telling them to chill out, have a party, don't accept responsibility for something they could not change. The strongest statement he made to them is one I use all the time when I'm thinking about being down and out: "The joy of the LORD is your strength" (NIV). If you can't think of anything else to tell your friends and family when things are going wrong, encourage them to find strength in the joy of the Lord. And laugh a little. It works for me!

One of the old hymns of the church reminds us to count our blessings by naming them one by one. We are to count our blessings and see what God has done. We can be encouraged when we are tossed to and fro by the winds of turmoil, the hail of despair, the clouds of depression, and the thunder of anger. An attitude of gratitude will always produce an attitude of praise, joy, and laughter. Praise works every day and every night, three hundred and sixty-five days a year. Try being thankful for twenty-one days and see if you don't begin to feel like singing praise to God, even if you just make a joyful noise. As the old commercial said, "Try it; you'll like it."

↝ *Lord, our gratitude cannot be fully expressed for all you do for us. Please accept our praise. And Lord, help us learn to laugh a little more. Amen.*

Laughing Later
NICOLE JOHNSON

ᜭ ❋ ᜭ

A time to weep and a time to laugh.
(ECCLESIASTES 3:4 NIV)

*L*aughter definitely has a latent side. Humor is almost always present in most life situations, but we can't always see it in the moment. Especially in the midst of our trying circumstances, as when we are frustrated or inconvenienced, we can miss the humor completely. Many times a friend has helped me by saying, "You'll laugh about this later." And she's usually right. But in the midst of it, I find myself thinking, *This is not funny*, which can be just another way of saying, "This is not funny to me *right now*."

Many times I don't find the humor in a situation until I look back on it. I suppose that's what wisdom would call *perspective*, giving me the understanding that the big deal at the time is really not such a big deal, or that the seriousness of my situation is multiplied when I take myself too seriously in the midst of it. Sometimes this perspective arrives within minutes, sometimes hours, depending on the depth of the situation. Or sadly, sometimes it takes years. I much prefer the comedy to surface quickly, as it has a way of reducing the pain and lightening the load.

This was exactly my experience several summers ago as I set off on an adventure to England to write for a week and do some research on castles for the book I was working on. It was an exciting and scary time for me as I was traveling abroad alone to a country I'd never visited before. I was working on the manuscript for *Keeping a Princess Heart in a Not So Fairy Tale World*, and I was about to discover just how difficult that would be.

From the minute I arrived, nothing went right. Except the word *right*. Which usually means something has gone wrong. Actually, it's the only word you need to know if you ever visit England. It can mean anything, but its most common translation in England is, "I couldn't care less."

Upon my arrival I followed the signs to baggage claim and waited for my luggage to appear. My overstuffed black cases contained my books, printer, and all the things I needed to continue working on the book—chocolate, music, candles—you know, important stuff. After waiting at the baggage carousel until the next flight's luggage started arriving, I approached the man behind the service counter. He was busy working on something, and I hated to interrupt, but I did, saying, "Excuse me, sir, my bag wasn't on the plane."

He said, "Right."

"Does that mean you don't know where it is?"

"Right."

"So that must mean you don't know when it will be coming?"

"Right."

"So I should leave the airport and drive two hours north without it?"

"Right."

There was not one change of expression in his voice or on his face the entire conversation. (Can it be called a conversation if he only spoke four words?) I suppose the English have so much history on their side that they just don't worry about the rest of us. They take their time with anything and everything. It's not that they don't sweat the small stuff; it's that they don't sweat *period*. If you discover you're on the wrong road, it could take you years to turn around. And because of their "roundabout" traffic circles, you really go around and around and around. I'm convinced they want to make Americans throw up on their first visit, so they won't stay long or ever come back.

My first challenge was the rental car. I sat behind the wheel on the driver's side for a long time trying to familiarize myself with the completely foreign dashboard. To tell you the truth, I was scared to death. I had great potential of hurting myself, not to mention some other unfortunate innocent soul who happened to be on the road that day. My little rental car was in grave danger, too, along with every hedge on the left side of England.

When I started the car, the windshield wiper on the back

window came on. I couldn't figure out how to turn if off. I tried everything I could think of to get it to stop, but to no avail. After sitting there a while, I thought I should be on my way as I was only staying in the country for a week. The car didn't move immediately. This little car, like a smart horse, knew that I was afraid of it, and it was acting stubborn.

I proceeded to the exit without hitting anything and gave the guy my license. He started laughing uncontrollably and said he'd seen me driving through the parking lot.

I'm certain he'd seen my type before—sweaty, nervous, and slightly green. And the back windshield wiper was a dead give-away that I was not in control of the situation. I asked him for directions, but unfortunately, I couldn't understand a word he said. Which led to another fit of laughing as he sputtered something about plain English.

He was having fun, but I failed to see the humor in that moment. I thought about turning in my car and trying to take a cab two hours north to Oxford, but there was no way to back up without puncturing the tires; so I gave the little car a good swift kick of gas, and the reluctant automobile went forward as uncertainly as I did.

Now behind the wheel, I was officially on the wrong side of everything natural to me—kind of like how I felt when I first moved to California, or what it feels to try to write with my left hand, or what happens to me when I don't get coffee in the morning. After one hundred yards I wanted to pull off, just to stop the shaking, but before I knew it, I was circling in one of those awful roundabouts. It took me three times around to interpret the signs as cars were speeding in front of me and around me, above me and directly at me, coming from every conceivable direction. If I slowed down, I got honked at, and if I sped up, I got dizzy. I felt like a dumb blonde American girl trying to drive in England. And, that's exactly what I was.

Finally I came to a traffic light, and I could stop and take a few deep breaths. I was concerned about the car, which still didn't want to fully cooperate with me. The back windshield wiper was still slapping back and forth. And the radio had been on but had since found a signal, and I couldn't turn it off; so I just turned it down.

It was then that I smelled something burning. I frantically looked around but saw nothing. About this time the light turned green. I noticed the guy behind me honking and trying desperately to get my attention. By now I was accustomed to this, so I didn't take it personally. I just kept driving forward, but slowly because the car was still hesitating. The car behind me pulled up alongside me telling me to roll down my window. It was then that I noticed that the parking brake was still on! I quickly released it and reached for the passenger window on the far left side (no automatic windows) and found how hard it is to put a window down with my left hand. I was driving on the right side with my right hand and reaching to Tasmania with my uncoordinated left hand. I got the window down just in time to hear him say cheerfully with his proper British accent, "Hallo. Did you know there's a fire in the back of your car?"

I'm sure I shook my head trying to say no, but I don't really remember. What I do remember saying was, "Thank you."

I had cars on either side of me, no place to pull off, a fire in the back of my car, a broken windshield wiper, and another traffic circle coming up! The fellow just waved cheerfully and drove on. The tears won out. I was sure the parking brake was what had caused the fire, but I was so scared, and I still had a couple of hours to go.

Needless to say, I made it. I never did get the windshield wiper to turn off, but by the time I got to the little village that would be my writing home for a week, I had begun to laugh about the whole thing. Not too long after the gentleman informed me of the fire, in the midst of my tears it had started to rain. And not just rain; pour! So when my already sketchy driving was compounded by lack of visibility from the rain inside and now out, I started to think the whole thing was pretty funny.

Then the thought crossed my mind that the rain would probably put out the fire, if it was still there; so I didn't need to pull over. And then I thought back over the guy aggressively waving to me, and how I ignored him because I thought he was peeved with my driving, and I chuckled. What must he have thought of my struggle to put the window down? I laughed some more. I was just a dumb blonde American girl trying to drive in England! When I accepted that, the scenario just got funnier and funnier. I remembered his asking me politely if I knew there was a fire in the back of my car, and I replied calmly, "Thank you," like yes, I knew, and that I keep it lit for toasting marshmallows or something.

And then I thought of the perfect response. When he told me there was a fire, I should have just looked at him calmly and said, "Right."

So I was only laughing, no more tears, when I finally arrived at my destination—especially upon seeing that Upper Slaughter was the actual name of the village. How appropriate. The sting of my fear and helplessness was gone with the recognition of the humor in my situation. I had no luggage, a burned-up car, and a bad case of the shakes. But being able to laugh, even though I couldn't in the moment it was happening, gave me back the joy that I felt being in England, on this exciting adventure.

Laughing defies difficult circumstances their thievery of your joy.

As I settled into the wonderful manor house that night, safe and sound, I thought, *It's no wonder that so many people come to England to get an education at Oxford or Cambridge. If they can drive there, everything else will be easy!*

So when it's raining on the inside and out, look for the humor that just may be hiding in your troubles. Laughing, even later, will release your heart and restore your joy.

Right!

↬   *O Father, teach us to laugh—at life's circumstances, at our troubles, at our pain, and especially at ourselves. Help us learn not to take ourselves so seriously and to look for joy in every nook and cranny. Help us, Lord, to laugh! Amen.*

The Moustache-Waxing Moments of Life

SHEILA WALSH

✤

She is strong and is respected by the people
She looks forward to the future with joy.
She speaks wise words and teaches others to be kind.
(PROVERBS 31:25–26 NCV)

*H*ave you ever noticed that aging is full of small indignities? I'm not talking about huge affronts or great mountains to scale, but rather the petty little bug bites of life that let us know we are not twenty or thirty or forty anymore. It might be the number of gray hairs that seem to be winning the color battle and now outnumber the rival brown or blonde ones. It could be the annoying fact that your lipstick seems preoccupied with heading north of your lip-line. It might be the mystery that, even if you weigh pretty much what you weighed ten years ago, clothes just don't seem to fit the same way any more—things have moved and your metabolism no longer does a tango but a very slow waltz! During the spring of 2005, my husband, Barry, and I decided to do something about that.

153

We purchased an elliptical exercise machine, which the salesman in the sports store assured us was the latest and best thing. It looks like a cross between a treadmill and a bike and even has a place to hold your bottle of water. I asked the salesman if it would also accommodate a large cup of coffee, but he seemed to think I was joking and never answered.

The machine was delivered in a truck, and two guys set it up in the bedroom. As they left, they handed me the manual, which made the Bible seem like a postcard. The bottom line, as far as I could tell after a quick scan, was that unless each session lasted at least forty minutes I would not be burning fat; I would just be getting my heart rate up. I disappeared into my closet and reappeared clad in sweatpants and my Women of Faith T-shirt. I stepped onto the pedals, and the electronic panel in front of me began to ask rather personal questions: How old are you? How much do you weigh? Do you know your fat-burning heart rate? Did you tithe last month? (I made that one up.)

I began my climb toward health. I programmed it for forty-five minutes and started pedaling. After some time I looked at the timer to discover that I had been on it for four minutes! I was exhausted. I managed to go for twenty and then fell off. As I lay on the carpet it told me that I had burned three hundred and fifty calories and had worked at my fat-burning heart rate for only 1.2 of the 20 grueling minutes! I have the stamina of an earthworm.

Last week I encountered a fresh indignity in the mystical world of aging as I sat in chair fourteen in my usual nail salon having my artificial nails filled. I don't really like having fake nails, but it is viewed by the men in my family as a gift to them. Barry and Christian love to have their backs scratched. They will sit with faces aglow, purring like cats with a bowl of fresh cream as I gently rake my claws up and down their spines. Last Christmas I had them removed to let my real nails breathe for a while and was greeted by stunned silence when I returned from the salon.

"What will we do now, Mom?" Christian asked.

"I thought about that!" I responded, jubilantly producing a back-scratcher that I purchased on my way home. Christian was not impressed.

"That won't work," he said.

"It will work," I assured him. "Let me show you how to use it."

"Mom, it won't work because it's not attached to you."

So I surrendered and have made peace with the fact that I will probably have to carry these ten beasts until the trumpet sounds.

The salon I frequent is a large one, and on this particular day every chair was taken. One or two women had said hello as I passed their chairs, acknowledging that they had previously attended a Women of Faith event.

As I sat with someone working on my nails and another on my feet, a new employee approached me and asked if I would like to have my eyebrows waxed. I politely declined because the last time I had that procedure done, it removed most of my forehead as well. With all the determination of a terrier, this girl was not going be left with idle hands and continued in a loud voice, "How about your moustache? Can I wax your moustache?"

"Moustache?" I said. "Moustache!"

I came home, and as I stared in the mirror, I realized that one of the gifts of God is that, as we age and things begin to grow on us, our eyesight begins to fade, too, so we remain blissfully unaware! That evening I asked Christian at dinner if he was aware that his mother had a moustache.

"Of course not, Mom!" he said laughing.

I was relieved but only for a moment.

"You don't have a moustache, but you do have a big hair growing out of the side of your face," he said. "Actually, you're quite a hairy person."

Barry rebuked *his* son for oversharing.

"I was just kidding about the hairy person bit, but the hair is there, Dad, honestly; look!" he said.

As I sat in the bath later that night reviewing my role as the missing link, something else occurred to me—I couldn't wait to tell Marilyn, Luci, Patsy, Mary, Nicole, and Thelma so that we could all enjoy a good laugh together. That's one of the great joys of friendship. We get to share our triumphs and tragedies, the unexpected joys, and the petty indignities of life. As I slathered on a little more lotion than normal that night, I thought of Solomon's words: "Just as lotions and fragrance give sensual delight, a sweet friendship refreshes the soul" (Proverbs 27:9 MSG).

We live in a culture consumed with looking younger and

younger all the time. If you check the latest batch of reality shows, they reflect our culture's obsession with perfection. In August 2002, *Time* magazine's Asian edition contained an article on South Korea's pursuit of the Western idea of beauty. Teenage girls as young as fourteen are popping into plastic surgery centers after school to have their eyes operated on. It's now the most popular graduation gift!

A 2004 report from *ABC News* disclosed that plastic surgery among the teenage population, specifically young females, was on the rise, and the breast implant procedure among the teen community was up 24 percent.

According to the American Society of Plastic Surgeons (ASPS) Web site, more than three hundred thousand cosmetic surgery procedures were performed on teens under the age of eighteen in 2003.

All of this makes me ask, where are we going as a culture, and what will distinguish God's children from those who don't know him? What I look for in my own life is balance and humor. I color my hair because I'm now probably 50 percent gray. I enjoy using makeup, although if you were to catch me at home you would see that I am just as happy with very little make-up and a ball cap on my head. I will turn fifty in 2006, and I'm comfortable in my own skin. Balance allows me to make some choices for myself without being defined by how I look or how others think I *could* look.

When we moved to Dallas from Tennessee, I was made aware again of how many in their thirties and forties take drastic measures to change or refresh their looks. Many of the moms in Christian's new school made efforts to make us feel at home, providing a meal or a fun day out for him, but one so surprised me with her welcome gift that I laughed out loud. She told me she had the list of all the best plastic surgeons in town. I told her that, if I was ever in a car accident and my face went through the windshield, I'd call her.

Balance is good, but humor is a lifesaver. As a team of speakers we are all different shapes and sizes—some are taller, some shorter, some younger, some not so young—but what we have as a bedrock of our friendship is that we love each other and laugh out loud at the moustache-waxing moments in life.

So that is my prayer for you today—that you may carve out a little time in your overcrowded schedule to laugh with your friends. If you find yourself in a friendless season, I hope you know that you have a Father who will gladly carry you and hold you through all the petty indignities of living in a fallen world. This body that we occupy for a few years is just a rental place after all. Our real home is with our Father, and it would seem to make sense that most of our time, energy, and money should be invested there, don't you think?

You are loved!

ᡐ *Dear Father, thank you for laughter and joy! May I be a source of hope and encouragement to my friends and family so that life will not seem so gloomy. And may I always find my wellspring of joy in you. In Jesus's name, amen.*

PART 6

❧

Joy Sings

Joy from the Ruins
Sheila Walsh
ꜱ ❋ ꜱ

Come, let's sing for joy to the LORD. Let's shout praises to the Rock who saves us. Let's come to him with thanksgiving. Let's sing songs to him because the LORD is the great God, the great King over all gods. The deepest places on earth are his, and the highest mountains belong to him. The sea is his because he made it, and he created the land with his own hands.

Come, let's worship him and bow down. Let's kneel before the LORD who made us, because he is our God and we are the people he takes care of and the sheep that he tends.

(Psalm 95:1–7 NCV)

I've just ordered an old CD of yours from eBay," Barry announced to me one morning.

"They are selling my CDs on an auction site?" I asked.

"Yes," he said. "I went online and typed in your name and all sorts of things came up. One lady is selling a letter you wrote to her, and there are signed pictures and T-shirts, tons of stuff."

"How weird is that!" I said. "Which CD did you order?"

"It's called *Shaddowlands*. The seller said she just listened to it once, so it's in good condition."

"That's not a good sign, Barry," I said. "If she just listened to it once, that isn't a huge vote of confidence. I hope you didn't pay much for it."

"No, it was going cheap!" he proclaimed with pride.

A few days later it arrived in the mail. It's a CD I recorded in England in 1986. I asked Barry if I could listen to it first, and he passed it over. I stuck it in the car CD player as I drove Christian to school that morning.

"Can you turn that down, Mom?" he asked.

On the return trip home, I listened to a little bit of each song. It's awful, worse than awful! It's not just that it's old and more trendy, because I made CDs before that one that I like, but it's the dumbest collection of songs I have ever heard. Not only that, but it reminds me of the old movie *Sybil* with Sally Field where she played a woman with multiple personalities. I sound like a different person on each song, as if I had to find a voice that would suit the song, rather than finding songs that suit my voice. I found myself traveling down memory lane trying to understand how I ended up at such a peculiar detour all those years ago.

When I was thirteen or fourteen years old, my school music teacher, Mrs. Cowan, singled me out for a solo during our school concert. I was terrified. The song was called "Cherry Ripe." I can still remember it. It's one of those tunes that buzz around your head like an annoying gnat long after you first hear it. Mrs. Cowan decided that I had some talent and entered me in the Ayrshire Music Festival, held annually in our town hall. I competed in the junior vocal solo class and the Burns competition (songs from our wonderful local poet Robert Burns), and I took first place in both.

Mr. Tweddle, a private music teacher, introduced himself to my mom and told her that he thought it would be worthwhile for me to take private lessons. Mum was a widow with three children and explained to Mr. Tweddle that she could not afford his fees; so for three years he taught me once a week for half price, and he gave me lessons that were twice as long as usual.

Mr. Tweddle and his wife were such dear people. After my lesson I would pop next door to the sitting room and have a cup of tea with Mrs. Tweddle, and we would talk and laugh about how eccentric Mr. Tweddle was. He would make me stand with my back pressed against the door and do my scales over and over, telling me that I sounded like a cross between a sheep and a machine gun. It was very hard for him when I graduated from high school and went to seminary. He so wanted me to pursue a career in opera, but I told him I wasn't fat enough to be an opera singer. When I went for my last lesson, I brought him a rosebush as a gift. He planted it in the yard just under the bay window where he sat at his piano.

I knew that God had called me to be a missionary. I thought then that I would end up in India with music far behind me, but God had other plans. While in school I was invited to join a band, something I gladly did because the drummer was so gorgeous. We sang in college campuses around the London area, and I began to see how powerful music is to communicate truth. As Mr. Tweddle's student I studied German lieder and opera, but now we sang about the living God. I had no idea, however, how I could serve God in a full-time capacity through music. In the United Kingdom we had no Christian radio stations or venues where Christian artists toured. But what seemed impossible to me was already planned out by my Father.

Just as I was about to graduate, I was invited to join a group called Oasis. This group was part of Youth for Christ's (YFC) outreach program, and they were based in Holland. For the next year we traveled all over Europe singing in schools and colleges, clubs and concert halls. Each member of the group was from a different country. I found that quite a lonely time in my life. I was the only native English-speaking one and although the others could speak English, they would often venture off into German or Dutch. The only German I knew was *"Heil Hitler"* and the only Dutch I knew was "Edam cheese!"

After my year was up, I went home to Britain and began working with British Youth for Christ as a school evangelist. (It's interesting to note that in Britain, which makes no claim of being a Christian country, I was able to go into classrooms and talk about Jesus, while here in America children struggle for the right to stand around the flagpole and silently pray.)

Each year in England, a Christian arts festival is held in August. My friends and I were invited to lead worship at the Sunday service. After the service I was approached by the head of a record label and asked if I was interested in recording. I found the thought very intimidating and told him that he would have to talk to my boss at YFC. Finally, plans were made, and I found myself caught up in a rapidly moving wave of change that took me all over the world and eventually dropped me off in America. The more opportunities I was given, the more complicated life became. I began singing because I loved it, but now there were other issues demanding attention—what songs would get radio play, what was happening in the secular scene that we could copy, how should I change the way I look to make me more acceptable to some who still thought of contemporary Christian music as dancing with the devil?

And so I found myself, thirty years old, in a studio with the dumbest collection of songs you have ever heard, written by people who were supposed to be the next big thing. For some time music lost all joy for me. It seemed commercial and heartless. I began cutting back, doing less and less. I never sang around the house or in the car. I was now the cohost of *The 700 Club* with Pat Robertson, and I pushed music further and further into the recesses of my soul.

Then one day everything stopped. From my privileged position beside Pat, I found myself falling and falling into a dark pit. I spent a month in a psychiatric ward with other patients who had lost their way, their purpose, and their joy. As I began to work with my doctor and receive treatment for clinical depression, the strangest thing happened to me. I was walking along the corridor from the cafeteria to my room one morning when I stopped and listened. I was singing. The sound coming from the ruins was different than I remembered. It was fragile but true, as if for the first time in my life I understood why we are given voices—to praise our Father in heaven. There was no thought of what is "in" or who I should sound like; it was the song of the free and redeemed, which is never out of tune or out of place.

Some people are given voices like nightingales that soar above all common sounds; most are given the song of the more ordinary bird. Whatever voice you have been given, I invite you today, right now, to lift it in praise to the Father, who sees you and loves you and delights in each joyful note.

  ~~ *O God, thank you for hearing my song, even when it came from the pits. Thank you for the power of music to teach, to heal, to encourage, and to create joy in the hearts of both the singers and the listeners. I love to sing your praises, Lord! Amen.*

A Greenroom Hallelujah!

MARILYN MEBERG

~ ✳ ~

Be glad in the LORD, and rejoice, you righteous,
and shout for joy, all you upright in heart. (PSALM 32:11 NKJV)

I love to eat! That is an amazing reality, simply because my mother used to pay me to eat. I was so skinny I looked as if I'd just crawled off a boat of refugees. I think my parents were a little embarrassed by my appearance. It could not help but reflect negatively on their images as competent parental caregivers.

Food was totally uninteresting to me and a burden to my day. It made no sense to stop what I was doing simply to engage in the consumption of something that had no appeal.

When I was dying to have a blue-and-white bike with a carrier on the back, my parents suggested I "eat for it." My friend Bev Withers also wanted a blue-and-white bike with a carrier on the back. Her parents suggested she "curb her eating" for it. (She

167

was a bit fluffy at the time.) In time, we each ate or didn't eat our way to new bikes. We celebrated by riding them the six miles to Campus Corner in Battle Ground. Bev had two chocolate milkshakes. I had a Butterfinger candy bar and a Coke.

I believe I was twelve or thirteen when it happened. My response to food totally changed. It was no longer burdensome or uninteresting. In fact, when Bev and I made our weekly bike trip to Campus Corner, I'd have a cheeseburger, fries, and a chocolate milkshake. Now, two hundred years later, if my mother had continued to pay me to eat, I'd be a wealthy woman.

One of my favorite food experiences I have with my Women of Faith Porch Pals is having dinner Saturday night after a conference. We share highlight experiences from the women we've talked to, giggle over each other's verbal missteps we hope no one heard, and then decide which desserts we may want to split. Patsy Clairmont and I have nearly identical food tastes; so we usually sit next to each other. (There have been times when I know she took more of my dessert than was an even split, but I'm such a gracious woman I rarely speak up.)

One of my specific food memories in relation to being with my Women of Faith buddies was when we walked into the greenroom (that's where speakers like us, or actors, or musicians hang out before we go onstage) for lunch on Saturday in a conference city. Quite frankly, the greenroom food is generally barely edible and serves the function of providing enough sustenance to merely get us through the rest of the day.

It isn't usually awful, but it skates close to that designation. On this particular Saturday, I was walking toward the room when suddenly I heard the jubilant sounds of the "Hallelujah" chorus. The joyful notes were charging out of the greenroom and zinging back and forth against the walls. It was being led by Babbie Mason. I thought to myself, *I could eat creamed wallpaper if it were accompanied by Babbie's voice.* Her choir was composed of all the Porch Pals, their assistants, our speaker guests, and the Integrity Singers. What a chorus! I quickened my steps. Something good was going on in the greenroom—there was joyful singing and there must be a good reason. Was there ever! Here's the scene that met my eyes. Spread out on a table with a white linen cloth and a fresh flower centerpiece was the following:

Platters of fried chicken (not soggy with grease)
Mounds of potato salad (not from Albertson's carton)
Fresh string beans (not canned or frozen but straight
   from Mr. McGregor's garden)
Fresh fruit salad with yogurt dressing
Cheddar cheese biscuits (light to the touch, not lethal if
   thrown)
Chocolate brownies with vanilla ice cream or apple pie
   with a crust Mrs. Dunbar could have made.

There was reason to sing for joy, and we did! It was amazing what deliciously prepared and aesthetically presented food did for our spirits. Since I'm always an after-lunch speaker, I know those chocolate brownies lifted me to new heights of verbal expression and spiritual inspiration.

For my birthday this past April, my "community" picked me up in a stretch limo and drove to an utterly exquisite French restaurant in Dallas. It was hard to control my squealing. I realized a muffled squeal implies distress, so I tried hard to just smile. But it was not easy to control my inclination to groan with pleasure over the herb-butter spread or moan at the taste of yeast rolls so flaky I was days getting them out of my sweater.

One of the greatest challenges to subdue my audible organic responses was when they placed a perfectly hollowed eggshell in front of us filled with a creamy, slightly cheesy, puddinglike substance I obviously can't identify. With a teeny-tiny spoon, we dipped into the delicate shell's contents and all went into simultaneous shrieks. Whatever it was, there are no words to describe it, but we knew it alone deserved a little praise service—some joyful singing. We didn't sing but should have just on the principle of rewarding the worthy.

Moses said in Deuteronomy 8:3, "Man does not live on bread alone" (NIV). He would have approved of my birthday dinner. We had so much more than bread alone. We also had that which characterizes my community: many laughs, great conversation, and the sure knowledge of the deep kinship and love we feel for each other. I believe one of God's gifts for not only the body but the soul is "bread" shared with each other in rich fellowship.

The Bible frequently refers to the celebratory role of food.

For example, when the prodigal son returned home, the father gave a feast. Why? His wayward son returned home to seek his father's forgiveness. It was perhaps too much to hope to be reinstated to the rights of membership in the family since Eastern custom dictated a father disown a son who showed such disrespect. According to custom, the boy should not have been allowed on the property, but contrary to expectation, the son was forgiven by his father and welcomed home. There was joyful singing, eating, and celebrating, not the prodigal's behavior but the father's forgiveness and the family's reunion.

Celebrating is one of the great instincts of human nature. I believe that's a God-given instinct. Revelation says when we open our heart's door to him, he'll come in and eat with us. Note these celebratory images in Revelation 3:20–21:

> Look! Here I stand at the door and knock. If you hear me calling and open the door, I will come in, and we will share a meal as friends. I will invite everyone who is victorious to sit with me on my throne, just as I was victorious and sat with my Father on his throne. (NLT)

Also the book of Revelation speaks of the great wedding feast we will all experience in heaven.

I love the call to joyful exuberance we read in Psalm 32:11. It says, "Be glad in the LORD and rejoice, you righteous, and shout for joy, all you upright in heart!" We might want to caution ourselves about not shouting for joy if our mouth is full. But on the other hand, I imagine I'm the only one who would be troubled by that. I have a feeling God receives our joyful singing with or without particles of food in our teeth.

Hallelujah!

 ∂ *Father God, as we sit in the green room of heaven, preparing to spend eternity with you, help us to enjoy all the wonderful things you give us right here on earth. You are the Great Provider, and we are the joyful recipients. Thank you, Father. We love you. Amen.*

Love Fills Your Heart with Joy
Thelma Wells
ᴚ ✳ ᴚ

Love the LORD with all your heart and with all your soul
and with all your strength.
(Deuteronomy 6:5 NIV)

I got a letter awhile back giving me some information and asking for my advice. This happens every day. I guess my gray hair qualifies me to be the mother confidant of thousands of people all over the world. As confidant, I cannot reveal who the letter was from, and I must change some of the facts so you smart people won't be able to figure out who it is. But I do want you to hear the gist of the letter and my suggestions. I try never to give advice, just strong suggestions that include my experience, my opinions, and the Word of God. This is the letter:

Dear Thelma,

My name is Mrs. So N. So, mother of seven. I am studying for my second degree. I come from a background of physical, mental, spiritual, and sexual abuse as a child. I've worked through a bunch of this with Christian counselors, as well as other counselors and professionals.

I accepted Christ in my teens, went to a Christian college, graduated, and worked in social services and governmental agencies. My husband and I have been married for over twenty-five years.

Thelma, I know that God comes in to stay when we ask, according to Revelation 3:20, and doesn't go bopping out. I have enough miracles in my life to prove this. I've had my share of spiritual attacks just like anyone else, but I had one I wasn't prepared for and didn't have my shield of faith up for. I picked up my Bible one day and all of a sudden I heard this: "You don't love God." Well, let me tell you, that threw me for a loop! There are times that I have to force myself to believe that God exists. I need help Thelma; I am sick of living like this.

Any help you can give me would be greatly appreciated (the sooner the better).

Sincerely,
Mrs. So N. So

This struck an emotional and spiritual cord with me, because many of the women I talk with daily are in the same situation. They think God has either left them, or they wonder if he really exists. These people, for the most part, have grown up in the church, accepted Christ at an early age, and have examples of faith to give them hope, but they still wonder about God, his promises, and his mere existence. I believe a great cause of this kind of thinking comes from our not knowing who we are in Christ. Even in my mentoring program, Daughters of Zion Leadership Mentoring Program, women come to me with their doubts and questions about God's existence and certainly his love for them.

Before the foundation of the world, God was. And he had established how his creation would live. He had planned for every animal, seed from the ground, angel, and human being to live in the fullness of his glory. He would extend his glory to us, and we would always do, say, and think the right way. Adam and Eve were the recipients of this glory. The reason they didn't know they were naked is because they were covered with the glory of God. All the animals got along with each other. There were no mosquitoes biting people, no killer whales swallowing people, no bumblebees stinging people. No people were getting food poisoning or getting colds and flu. People were not even getting sunburned. And there was nothing to fear in all the earth.

That all changed instantly when Eve ate the forbidden fruit and Adam gave in to her and ate it too. The glory of God left them, and their bodies were exposed as naked and something to be covered. Pain and suffering, sickness and disease, grief and sorrow, evil and sin became a part of the daily dilemma of life. Where did the glory go? It went back to the Glory-giver, God. On special occasions, he still allowed it to come down to earth to certain people who had proved they loved him and honored his name.

God's real desire for us is to be filled with his glory every day in every way. That's why, after allowing people to suffer, be enslaved, and go through tremendous agony, he sent the glory back to the earth. Glory came down in Jesus Christ—the only begotten Son of the omnipotent God. Jesus could have come back as a grown man or as a king highly exalted, but if he had he would not have been able to rescue us from the bondage of sin. Jesus was able to do that because he was born of a woman, lived as any other human, ministered to people according to the Jewish customs of that day, suffered a cruel death on an old rugged cross, was buried in a borrowed tomb, was raised from the dead on the third day, walked among us so eyewitnesses could see for themselves that he was alive again, and ascended to his Father in heaven to sit at his right side and make intercession for us. He brought the glory down and left it for us, to display all the days of our lives, in sickness and in health, in sorrow and in wealth, until death takes us.

Knowing and believing in Jesus is the only real joy in this land. Getting to know Jesus acquaints us with God. Applying what we learn about Jesus and continually partaking of his Word creates his glory in us, and thereby we are able to let our light shine among men so they can see his glory in us. Glory is the fullness of God in us, the abundance that he promised us, the contentment he gives us, and the peace that abides in us.

One of the most powerful ways of getting over the turmoil of the circumstances in our lives is to fall madly in love with Jesus. How do you do that? Just as you pursue a man, you would pursue Jesus through prayer, Bible study, and praise.

Prayer is the key that unlocks the door to God's heart. Saying the Lord's Prayer with meaning is one of the most powerful prayers you can pray. When you don't know what to say, just say, "Jesus!" Not profanely but in reverence. "Jesus!"

You can read and listen to the Word of God and be absorbed in the Word. If you don't understand the Bible when you read it, may I suggest that you purchase The Message version by Eugene Peterson. This Bible is written in contemporary prose so we can understand the Bible better. If you don't have a lot of time to read the Bible, I suggest you get a set of Bible tapes or CDs and play them in your home and car. There's no excuse for not getting the Word of God into your mind in this technology-savvy world.

Praising God through song and dance is another way to get your spirits up and keep them up. When we begin to praise God, God begins to sing and rejoice over us. Awesome!

Worship God for who he is, not for what he can do for you. When you worship God in spirit and truth, you will feel his presence with peace you cannot understand. The result is that you will develop a love for God that you didn't know you could have. You will stop concentrating on the past, problems, or possibilities, and begin to concentrate on the Problem Solver.

Give God your frustrations, anger, bitterness, loneliness, hurts, disappointments, and heartaches, and watch him begin to heal you. In the process of healing, do something good for someone who cannot do anything in return for you. Forgive those who may have harmed you. Stop talking about your problems and relinquish them to God. You will be improving every day when you continually do these things. Before you know it, you won't have to say, "Ouch." You can be singing for joy!

One day, I was going through turmoil in my life. I asked God to give me something to do or say every time I thought of this situation. It was something I could not fix on my own. In my heart when I asked God, he led me to say this each time my problem came to my mind: "Jesus, Jesus, Jesus." That's it. Say, "Jesus, Jesus, Jesus." I did and I still do. The result is, as quickly as I call his name, my thought processes are brought under his command, and I don't think about the turmoil anymore.

When you call the name Jesus, glory returns to your mind and you can see the results. When you call the name Jesus, you are calling on the Word of God and the name of God at the same time. The most unique thing happens when you call the Word and the name Jesus—joy fills your heart!

In the middle of your sorrow, pain, anger, bitterness, hopelessness, poverty, shame, guilt, homelessness, joblessness, abuse, depression, and agony, joy can return to your spirit by calling on the name of Jesus. There is no other name under the heavens that can give you such sweet relief than Jesus—the sweetest name I know! Jesus loves you and fills your heart with joy.

Jesus, every time I call your name you prove your love for me in such a sweet way. Thank you for allowing me to even speak your name. When we are in turmoil, remind us of what to say and who you are. Amen.

Hit Parade

PATSY CLAIRMONT

~ ✳ ~

Make a joyful noise unto the LORD. . . . (PSALM 100:1 KJV)

I sing a lot. And even though my gift is not mercy in the musical arena of my life, I spare the public my singing performances. They don't generate joy, trust me. But I do love tapping my toe and belting out my favorites when I am boot-scootin' around my house. Usually singing as I vacuum works well, as the motor drowns out the most offensive parts. And I do let loose at the Women of Faith conferences while tucked between my Porch Pals, who have learned to just nod and smile at me. Or were those grimaces? Anyway, I love music.

Once I did sing in public, at least that is what I'm told. I have totally blocked the occasion out of my recall. Professionals tell us that we do that if a memory is too painful to remember. This one must have been a doozy. The report that this occurred came from an undeniable source—the other half of the duet, my friend Edith. And if I remember correctly, she wouldn't tout singing as one of her stronger gifts either. But the story goes that we had returned from a weekend retreat and wanted to teach our church the new song we had learned. It was a small church, but not small enough to deserve *us*, I'm sure. Here is how you know if people really love you: when you do something way outside your ability, and they still welcome you to sit next to them in the church pew on Sunday.

The one I sat next to on a regular basis and who was my all-time-favorite singer was my mom. It's not that she had a great voice (the apple doesn't fall far from the tree), but I gleaned a lot about Jesus from the songs that she sang as she went about her daily routine in our home. Whether she was making beds, doing laundry, or cleaning up the kitchen, she was singing. For me, it was like taking courses in the life of Jesus. I learned I have a friend in him, that if I walked and talked with Jesus I would have joy, that his promises would give me a solid place to stand, that I had a mansion just over the hilltop, and when I needed refuge I could run to him.

I can still see my mom opening windows on a summer's day, blonde hair bouncing gently, her apron-clad dress stirring in the breeze, as she sang, "He lives! He lives! Christ Jesus lives today. . . ." Suddenly the air in our home was pure with praise. There was no doubt for those of us who lived with her that Mom's faith was heaven sent.

Mom joined heaven's choir last year, and I can't begin to

imagine the extent of her joy. Her last ten years on earth were muddled with Alzheimer's, and she eventually lost the words to her beloved hymns. On one occasion I sang some of Mom's favorites to her over the phone to see if I could bring her back even for a few minutes from the clouded pit she had fallen into. After a few choruses, I asked her if she remembered them and Mom said "no" but that I had a "nice voice." I knew then that she was in real trouble. But now her recall is perfect, as is her pitch, and her joy is seam-splitting full.

My mom's voice, and more importantly the truths of those hymns, are part of my DNA. I can't tell you how often the words of songs she sang make their way across my mind to boost my lagging spirit and redirect my feet to God's path. So those of you with great voices and those of you with "joyful noises" sing, sing, sing . . . you never know who is listening and recording every note or when God will replay those truths for them.

I often think how blessed we are to have the lyrics of David's songs. What would we do without the hymnal of the book of Psalms? For even the world has bowed its head in reverence to his lyrics in Psalm 23: "The LORD is my Shepherd; I shall not want," as well as, "Yea, though I walk through the valley of the shadow of death, I will fear no evil; for you are with me." And what about the reassurance of the words he penned to this song: "The LORD is my rock and my fortress and my deliverer; my God, my strength, in whom I will trust" (Psalm 18:2 NKJV).

My life verse comes from Psalm 1:3, which says, "He shall be like a tree planted by the rivers of water, that brings forth its fruit in its season, whose leaf also shall not wither, and whatever he does shall prosper" (NKJV).

Years ago when hi-fi and record albums were in, I had an album by Little Jimmie Dickens (you have to have country leanings or watch the Grand Ole Opry to know him), and on that album he sang words from "my" psalm, "Just like a tree planted by the waters I shall not be moved," he'd shout. I, in response, would bounce all over my house belting those words out with him. (Which could explain why my neighbors all bought dogs.) But there's just something about singing that ignites bounce (actually today for me it's more like jiggle, yet nonetheless music and words are definitely joy enhancers).

And someone who knew that to be true was the King. No, not Ol' King Cole—he already was a merry soul with his three fiddlers, but I'm referring to Ol' King Saul. Cranky Saul often called for David, then a shepherd boy, to play and sing for him, to soothe his unsettled mind. Saul had sinking spells that could only be relieved by David's music.

I understand that. I cannot count the times over the years when my helium would leak out and the Lord would bring me a message through a song to re-inflate my joy. So many of those were directly from the Psalms. Years of living with exaggerated fears often caused me to battle back with, "The LORD is my light and my salvation; whom shall I fear? The LORD is the strength of my life; of whom shall I be afraid?" (Psalm 27:1 NKJV). And hope was (and is) my theme song when I sang, "He brought me up also out of a horrible pit, out of the miry clay, and he set my feet upon a rock, and established my goings" (Psalm 40:2 ASV). Even now it's hard for me to write that stanza without lifting my voice and singing hallelujah!

Number one on my Psalm Hit Parade is the One Hundredth Psalm. I memorized it as a child, and it still fills me with holy pleasure. I love the triumphal procession as worshipers make their way into his gates to praise the Lord: "Make a joyful noise unto the LORD all ye lands, come before his presence with singing…"

David could not have written such a diversity of musical themes had he not first tested his lyrics in the waters of his life. He knew enemies—fierce ones starting with the lions and bears that he fought and triumphed over when they attacked his sheep. Why, even those who loved him turned against him, like King Saul, who conspired repeatedly to have David killed. And once David became king of Israel, his enemies increased to include nations who fought against him.

Probably David's most known enemy was the giant Goliath. Today Goliath would be of prime-time interest to the sponsors of "Big Time Wrestling." He was a Philistine (enemies of Israel) and he was over nine feet tall. Now that's a lot of enemy. Add to that the fact that he was a seasoned warrior and was garbed in all the latest battle technology—a suit of mail, a bronze helmet, and, get this, he even had a shield-bearer who went before him. Goliath was impressive, intimidating, and full of himself. He thought he was invincible, but into the valley steps David—a shepherd, songwriter, singer, and musician—and with the swift rhythm of a gazelle he runs forth, swings his sling, and fells the giant man of war. Songs have been written about that up-close-and-personal encounter ever since.

Yes, no doubt about it, David's music will go on to resound in the halls of eternity, and to think—it all began in a shepherd's field with the background music of bleating sheep. To impact the world, God used a young, inexperienced man but one who had a listening ear, a willing heart, and a courageous spiri . . . now that should be joyful music to our ears!

I can't sing, but I can listen; I may not know how to harmonize, but I'm willing to try, and I may quiver when asked to step into a valley and face my "giant," but I have learned to run forth singing, "Onward, Christian soldiers…"

Thanks, Mom!

And thanks, Father, for the marvelous gift of music. It brings joy to my soul and hope to my heart. I love to praise your matchless name in happy songs and hymns, for you, Lord, are the song of my life. Amen.

Singing My Heart Out to God

LUCI SWINDOLL

ᔇ ✳ ᔇ

I'm singing my heart out to GOD . . .
GOD *is my strength,* GOD *is my song, and yes!*
GOD *is my salvation.* (EXODUS 15:1–2 MSG)

A couple of years ago, I was in the British Airways airport lounge in London thinking about a long flight home and not feeling very well. I had laid my head back on the overstuffed chair in which I was sitting and closed my eyes. To tell you the truth, I was dreading the nine-hour flight home when I began to hear someone whistling that old hymn "Day by Day." Because I love it and have sung it so many times, I knew most of the words by heart and let them scroll through my mind as the person whistled:

Day by day and with each passing moment,
Strength I find to meet my trials here;
Trusting in my Father's wise bestowment,
I've no cause for worry or for fear.

On and on they came to mind until I had virtually sung every word of the first verse in my head, accompanied, of course, by the stranger's tune. When I opened my eyes, I saw the person who was whistling. It was Geraldo Rivera, the TV news personality. Although he was several feet away from me, I think I stared at him. Why? Well, first of all, it felt odd to see someone I recognized so up close and personal. Second, I couldn't believe he and I were in that lounge at the same time. And third, what was *he* doing whistling a *hymn?*

While I was at it, I asked myself other questions: *Does Geraldo find strength day by day in the Savior? Does he trust what that tune affirms? Did God send him in here to "whistle a happy tune" just for me because he knew I needed those words of comfort just at this moment?* (It's very easy for me to have running conversations with myself. I do it all the time. It probably comes from living alone!)

Joy sings to us from the most unexpected places. Ever notice that? Surely you've gone grocery shopping where music is coming through the loudspeaker and you know the tune. You start singing with the vocal artist and dancing down the paper towel aisle. Or you pick up a floor mop, and the two of you give it a whirl. (Maybe that's not quite you, but it's certainly me, and I've danced my way through the detergents with some mighty mean mops).

My favorite store musical happened in Nordstrom. I was shopping for a few Christmas gifts one evening, and the place was pretty crowded. I wanted to rush in and out without much fanfare or frenzy. Running late with my shopping and chiding myself about procrastinating, I wasn't in the best of Christmas spirits. But just as I walked in the door I heard piano music being piped all over the store.

I made my way to the handbag department and tried to decide between two billfolds as gifts. As I began to settle into shopping to the strains of the music, I realized that sandwiched between pieces like "Have Yourself a Merry Little Christmas" and "Rudolf the Red-Nosed Reindeer," there were also familiar hymns I'd heard all my life. Great doctrinal pieces like "A Mighty Fortress Is Our God" and "Jesus, the Very Thought of Thee" and "Praise the Savior, Ye Who Know Him!" Every third or fourth song was one of those hymns. I loved that. They were being played in such a mellow, beautiful, slow fashion, you couldn't tell they were hymns unless you knew that in advance. After a bit, "O Come All Ye Faithful" was played—one of the greatest Christmas hymns of the faith. It wafted across the floor in all its harmonies and before I knew it, I was quietly singing those familiar words that Frederick Oakeley wrote in 1841:

O come, all ye faithful, joyful and triumphant,
O come ye, O come ye to Bethlehem.
Come and behold Him, born the King of angels!
O come, let us adore Him, O come, let us adore Him,
O come, let us adore Him, Christ the Lord!

When I got to the second line, a woman with a nice soprano voice, shopping about three feet away joined in, so I switched to the alto part. We never looked up; we just kept singing and milling through the aisles sort of lost in our own worlds but not missing a note or a word. Shop-girl duet!

After the first verse was sung, the pianist kept playing, modulating to a higher key on each verse, and we modulated right along with her. Then a gentleman and his wife walking by with Christmas packages heard us, so they stopped and joined in. We had a quartet going! By now, we'd all looked up at each other, and everybody was smiling . . . and still singing. How could we have known the bass was a shoe salesman passing by with five or six boxes of pumps in his arms? *Hello!*

Wow! Was this fun, or what? Before long, we'd sung every verse in full harmony, everybody in the vicinity had joined in whether they could actually carry a tune or not, and the handbag department had been converted into a scene from Charles Dickens, without the costumes, of course. As it turned out, the pianist happened to be somebody who went to my church. This was old home week! We had our own chorus, accompaniment, vocal sections, and applause. I loved it so much I actually stopped hurrying.

Joy sings!

How often does something like this come along to lift us out of our ordinary, mundane lives, but in our haste, we miss it? The author Hermann Hesse says, "Where we find something that resembles music, there we must stay; there is nothing else worth striving for in life than the feeling of music, the feeling of resonance and rhythmic life, or a harmony that justifies our existence."

I grew up in a singing family and can't remember a time somebody wasn't singing, playing piano, listening to music on the radio, or involved in the school chorus or church choir. Music. Music. Music. All of it laid down a rich bed of memories against which I now evaluate and absorb other music that comes my way. Each layer adds to the richness of my experience and helps me recall many joyful musical times in my childhood.

I remember songs my mother taught me that she had sung in the 1920s and '30s. I call them to mind at the weirdest times, and they come alongside my everyday life to lift me to another plane. Three years ago I heard one of them in Antarctica, after possibly sixty years of it lying silent in that "rich bed of memories." It's "The Umbrella Man," and I somehow recalled every single word of it and sang it as I danced with an engaging, handsome gentleman in Port Lockroy—an old British postal station. How remote is that? A *forever* memory!

And in 2004, as part of my Women of Faith message during the Irrepressible Hope conference, I sang another song learned when I was a pre-teen. The song "Egyptian Ella" has wonderful, funny, charming lyrics, and it fit perfectly with what I was trying to convey to the audience. In fact, the whole story of finding the music after several decades of no reason to look for it is a fascinating saga in itself.

A friend of mine Googled "Egyptian Ella" and came up with a Web site of a songwriter named "Perfesser Bill." She hit on his Web page and actually located the music, a soundtrack that could be purchased. She and Perfesser Bill Edwards became e-pals, writing back and forth, establishing a sweet bond. By the time I got involved and began e-mailing him myself, we had found out all sorts of interesting things about this extraordinary man and his family.

Not only did he play piano and ukulele, but he was a Christian composer, a church pianist, and it "just so happened" all the women in his family attended Women of Faith conferences—his wife, mother, daughters, and daughter-in-law. I'll tell you, when we learned that, we hadn't hit a Web page; we'd hit a goldmine! We were out of our heads—yelling, carrying on, and singing Handel's "Hallelujah" chorus. Perfesser Bill was a Woman of Faith *guy* in every sense of the word. And we'd learned about all this through the joy of singing.

There seems to be no end to that joy!

The first few verses of Exodus 15 talk about singing. They're the words of Moses as he and the Israelites sang to God, giving voice together: "I'm singing my heart out to GOD . . . GOD is my strength, GOD is my song, and yes! GOD is my salvation" (Exodus 15:1–2 MSG).

This is the greatest way of all that joy can sing—to God, in praise and thanksgiving. As we sing our hearts out to God, he increases our joy and happiness. He gives us the "feeling of resonance and rhythmic life." He gives us "harmony that justifies our existence."

ᔓ *Heavenly Father, thank you for the glorious gift of music! I can't imagine my life without the joy of praising you in song, lifting your name on high, and hearing it dance among the clouds on notes and rhythms that you alone can inspire. Hallelujah! Amen.*

PART 7

❧

Joy Encourages

Mansions and Bridges
Luci Swindoll

~ ✳ ~

We trust in the name of the LORD our God.
(PSALM 20:7 NIV)

Sometimes I don't take God at his Word. Simply put, I just do not believe him. Interestingly, unbelief kills my joy. For example, his Word says, "Ask and it will be given to you; seek and you will find; knock and the door will be opened to you" (Matthew 7:7 NIV). That's true whether I believe it or not. But when I don't believe it, I find myself exceedingly discouraged.

I had lived in an apartment my entire adult life when, in 1990, I realized an apartment no longer accommodated my lifestyle. Having seen a lovely area of condominiums not far from my old and dilapidated apartment, I wandered through its gates one afternoon, looked around, and thought, *Lord, I would love living here.* I weighed all the challenges confronting me, prayed to high heaven, and asked for the counsel of my closest friends. In spite of their tremendous encouragement to go ahead, I felt afraid. So I did nothing.

A few days later I was bemoaning my fate to Mary Graham, one of my dearest friends, and she said as assuredly as I've ever heard her, "Luci, I believe you can move in there. What's holding you back? Let's figure it out. We'll all help you. Let's trust God to open the door." *Yeah, right, sweet Mary.*

She and I went to the manager of those condos and were told I could lease one for a year if I could work something out with an owner who might not be living there during that time. After lots of looking, waiting, weighing all the options, I finally found a one-bedroom that I thought might fill the bill. It had a very adequate kitchen, a tiny patio, small bedroom and a two-car garage. I told the woman I'd take it and went away for a week of work with my brother's Insight for Living ministry.

I was so excited I could hardly wait to move. I asked Mary if she'd keep tabs on the process while I was gone. She called one afternoon to tell me the owner decided not to lease after all; the deal had fallen through, and the condo would not be mine. I was heartsick and, ultimately very depressed. I remember crying, pouting, and thinking things like, *I didn't deserve it anyway. Who am I to have a place like this? Get used to it, Luci, you're destined to live in that apartment all your life, no matter what.* I didn't pray or hope, much less "ask or seek or knock."

But Mary didn't give up. The minute that first place fell through, she started praying and believing God for another one. She knocked on doors, made phone calls, read the want ads, and, in the meantime, added my name to the prayer lists of a few of her friends. When I was rock bottom, she was up. When I was sad, she was happy. When I was discouraged, she encouraged me. It was *her* joy that kept me going. I was very downhearted. As my voice teacher used to say, "I could have put on a silk hat and walked under a duck."

By the time I returned from my trip, Mary had a lead on another place in the same community. But before checking it out, the manager looked me straight in the face and said, "Well, I'll tell you Luci, the owner and his wife don't actually live here, because they've built a house and have just moved into it, but he's an absolute pain in the neck. *Nobody* in the complex likes him, even though his wife is very sweet. He's strict and obsessed with rules and drives a hard bargain with all of us in management. But I'll be glad to put you in touch with him if you think it's worth a try."

Somewhat reluctantly, I said, "Well, yeah. What have I got to lose?" and agreed to meet with him. We set up a date and time, and with a bit of fear and trembling, I went to the appointed place and we met for the first time. Believe it or not, I loved the guy! I found him no more particular than I . . . and about the same things. It was a match made in heaven. And I loved his wife. Yes, he was strict, had lots of rules, and drove a hard bargain, but it didn't bother me. Gratefully, I noted that he'd kept his house exactly the way I would plan to keep it—clean and orderly.

The place was for sale at a price much higher than I could possibly afford, but after I told him my situation very honestly and asked if I could possibly lease the condo for one year, he agreed. It was beautiful: two-story with two bedrooms and two baths upstairs, a deck, an entire guest quarters downstairs with private bedroom and bath, living room, huge kitchen, and a large dining room I turned into a floor-to-ceiling library. Plus, there was a big patio overlooking a grassy knoll with giant, mature trees where birds roosted and sang all day long.

He agreed to lease at a price I could afford, and I was over the moon! My friend's joyful encouragement had made it possible for me not to give up, but to believe that God will lead if we trust him as we go. I put down a large deposit and began living in my dream condo, leased month to month. When I sent him my thirty-day payment, I always wrote him a letter to go with it. Each month I did that, never missing a single payment. I brought him up to date on what was going on in the complex, thanked him over and over for trusting me with his home, told him of any problem I faced in the unit, and the like. He loved that, and I loved reporting, both of us obsessing over the exact same details of life. As I said, I had met my match.

The owner, his wife, and I became friends, and in 1991 when he was put in charge of deploying military men and women into Desert Storm, I prayed for him and told him so. "Never," he said, "I mean *never*, Luci, has anybody prayed for me about anything. Thank you so much. I appreciate it more than you know. I'm sure your prayers will get me through this awful and demanding duty."

Each year the lease contract was renewed, and at the end of three years, I had opportunity to actually buy an affordable condo in Palm Desert, California, which I decided to do. I regretted having to tell my landlord and say good-bye to him and his wife. Not only did they wish me well and return all the deposit I made three years before, but they gave me an enormous basket of fruit, ham, sweets, breads, cheeses, and fancy crackers to send me on my way with their blessing. It was the size of the hood of my car! I cried when I saw it and bid them farewell. Long after I moved, I got calls from him asking if I would pray for him, or if he could use me as a reference for a job placement, or if I could come see him and his wife. He even called once to tell me he had a new address and wanted me to keep it in my Rolodex.

You know what I learned? Nothing is impossible with God. *Nothing!* Impossibility lies only in our minds, not in God's ways and means. We *have* not because we *ask* not. Occasionally I get caught in that old trap of not taking God at his Word . . . of thinking I have no one to trust but myself. Then, I remember God is my Father, my caregiver, and my caretaker. And I remember Mary, my encouraging joy giver. I remember that time I was at rock bottom and her joy pulled me up, and that wonderful homeowner and his generosity, even though I had been discouraged by the manager, who recommended I turn and walk away. I remember that opportunity to pray for somebody I barely knew and for whom nobody had ever prayed. I remember the privilege and thrill of believing God for something I had never believed could happen. And looking back on all that now, I'm reminded of how God's purposes are always greater than our own.

In fact, now I know that I leased that condo to teach me a

very important lesson about God. He means what he says, he keeps his word, he brings good news in spite of the bad, and he blesses way beyond what we could possibly ask or think. That's what he does best! And when I'm at my very worst, he keeps at it in spite of my shortsightedness. He's the king of joyful encouragement.

I wish these kinds of lessons weren't so hard to learn. I wish I'd just trust. Simply trust all the time. If I did, living in a mansion wouldn't be that different from living under a bridge.

~ *Father God, please forgive me for not believing you, trusting you, and taking you at your Word. Teach me to put my faith and my life in your hands—the king of joyful encouragement. I love you, Father. Amen.*

Mama T's Love for Mentoring

Thelma Wells

⁓ ✳ ⁓

The older women . . . can train the younger women.
(Titus 2:3–4 NIV)

*H*ave you ever wished for someone to take you under her wings, encourage you, and teach you everything she knows? Have you ever said you want a mentor in your life? Can you name the mentors in your life? How have you benefited from the mentors in your life?

These are valid questions asked every day by people throughout the world. People want to lean on, learn from, and latch on to those who have information and inspiration that can help them in their careers, ministries, communities, churches, and homes. I know, because not a week goes by without someone asking me to mentor them or teach them something.

We all long for affiliation and association from our families, friends, coworkers, communities, and church members. It's our nature. We want to belong to something, especially something that can enhance us to those from whom we can learn. The fact is we all have mentors in our lives who have encouraged us, taught us, and befriended us in one way or the other.

For some of us, our parents or guardians were our best mentors and encouragers. They taught us great and small life lessons that we will never forget and that we will practice all our lives. For example, when you cough, cover your mouth; when you sneeze, say "excuse me"; don't put your finger in the electrical socket because it may shock you; put your coat on before you go out into the cold air. Or study hard because an education is important, always tell the truth, breakfast is the most important meal of the day, and thousands more lessons that we sometimes take for granted.

For others of us, our mentors were coaches, teachers, pastors, grandparents, scout leaders, youth leaders, and the list goes on.

What is a mentor? A mentor is a teacher who comforts and confronts. She is committed, a confidant, caring, calm, and credible. She's a communicator, critical thinker, clean living, complimentary, challenging, and controlled. OK, so you may not be all that, but you qualify in at least one category.

Becoming a good mentor requires accountability.

The mentor and the one being mentored must be receptive to constructive criticism.

Mentoring requires trust and transparency.

Mentoring is a scriptural means of training people for maturity in their Christian walks. You can't go to the next level of maturity if you're not willing to leave where you are and move forward.

Mentoring requires a hunger and thirst to grow.

Mentoring was not structured to be easy training but a tool for developing lifelong disciplines. Mentoring requires mutual respect. Neither the teacher nor the student knows everything, but they can learn from each other. Eventually, the student should become a teacher, mentoring others and doing greater works.

Mentoring requires recognition of the talents and gifts of the one being mentored.

Mentoring is not designed so that you have someone to do your working, praying, and fasting *for* you, but someone who will pray and fast *with* you.

I know firsthand about mentoring. You see, in 2001 I started a leadership mentoring program in my home for ladies in my area. Ladies would stop me in the grocery store and ask if they could talk to me about their situations. Tons of e-mails were on my computer every week asking for instruction, advice, and opinions, telling me secrets, and begging for help. These people wanted a mother figure or someone who looked like they had lived long enough to have answers to some of life's most challenging problems.

Droves of women in the church are new converts to Christianity and are looking for someone to take them under their wings, encourage, and mentor them. I discovered from the cross section of women I've mentored that it doesn't really matter how long you've been going to church. You still have questions and are curious about things you've either heard or read and don't understand. Or you may have some personal issues that need airing and for which you need to get a biblical perspective. These issues can best be addressed by someone who has experienced the empowerment of being mentored and, in turn, the joy of being the mentor.

The church is one of the best places to create a mentoring atmosphere. There are young women who need guidance. There are married women who need advice. There are new converts who need to know what Christianity is all about.

Howard Hendricks talked about the necessity for good mentors this way: "The greatest crisis today is the crisis in leadership. And the greatest crisis in leadership is the crisis of character. Character is the result of four things:

1. The choices you make;
2. The values you embrace;
3. The crises you experience;
4. The mentor you choose."

The Old and New Testaments speak to the needs of people needing help. Proverbs ask these questions:

Wisdom shouts in the streets, she lifts her voice in the square; at the head of the noisy streets she cries out; at the entrance of the gates in the city, she utters her sayings: "How long, O naive ones, will you love being simple-minded? And scoffers delight themselves in scoffing, and fools hate knowledge? (1:20–22 NASB)

Remember, people can perish because they don't have knowledge (see Hosea 4:6). But not knowing in this information age in the world is no justification for perishing. There are churches on almost every corner. Yet, there are many people who still don't know how to live right. How long will they exist without knowledge? As long as we who know keep what we know to ourselves. As long as we are timid about speaking up and speaking out to women about things that matter. The New Testament declares,

Whatever is true, whatever is honorable, whatever is right, whatever is pure, whatever is lovely, whatever is of good repute, if there is any excellence and if anything is worthy of praise, let your mind dwell on these things. (Philippians 4:8 NASB)

Great advice, but how can you ponder what you don't know? Only by *teaching* the right way can people *know* the right way.

There is a mandate in the Bible for women to become mentors. This is partly the reason I became a mentor. It reads,

Older women likewise are to be reverent in their behavior, not malicious gossips nor enslaved to much wine, teaching what is good, so that they may encourage the young women to love their husbands, to love their children, to be sensible, pure workers at home, kind, being subject to their own husbands, so that the word of God will not be dishonored. (Titus 2:3–5 NASB)

Becoming a mentor who encourages people in your church is not easy, because it requires commitment and dedication, but the rewards are phenomenal. A mentor has these characteristics:

- Maturity;
- God-honoring behavior;
- Does not gossip or speak evil against others;
- Must not be a drunkard;
- Must teach what is good;
- Must encourage the young women to love their own husbands;
- Must teach them to love their children;
- Must teach them to have common sense;
- Must keep their houses clean;
- Must be kind; and
- Must be subject to their own husbands.

These are just the basics if you want to be an effective mentor. If you qualify under the guidelines of Titus 2, let's make it happen.

One of the first things I did was to invite ladies to my house for an informal dinner meeting to see how many were interested in being mentored. Out of fifty invitations, more than forty ladies came. Out of the forty ladies, twenty-seven of them leaned, learned, latched on to the program, and graduated after nine months of study. The same happened the next year and the next. Some of these ladies have started their own mentoring groups. Others are coming back for Phase II, the second tier to the mentoring program.

One thing a mentoring program can do is to build relationships. To be a successful mentor, you must have vision, a mission, and passion. Each mentoree is looking to gain knowledge, strength, wisdom, and skills. If there is no passion for the task, it shows, and the mentoring relationship is altered.

The greatest joy of a teacher is seeing the light of understanding in the students' eyes and watching them bear godly fruit.

My gray hair gives me enough credibility to be called Mama T by thousands over the world whom I've seen and whom I've never seen but have mentored over the years. I always encourage them by reminding them of my motto: "In Christ, you can BEE your best!"

↝ *Holy Father, thank You for the charge to influence, encourage, inspire, and empower people to BEE their best for you. Help me to always be strong and committed to the task of mentoring that You have given me. In Jesus's name, amen.*

A Christmas to Remember
MARY GRAHAM
჋ ✳ ჋

Do not worry about your life . . . (MATTHEW 6:25 NIV)

$\mathcal{I}$t was Christmas morning, and there wasn't a single gift in the house. When my three brothers and I awakened, there was nothing reflecting the season except a slightly dying, sparsely decorated little tree that Mrs. Cronk, the fifth grade school teacher, had given us when school got out for the holidays. The living room was so small that even that little scrawny tree, as pitiful as it was, seemed like an intruder.

"Joy to the World" was being sung on the radio that morning, but there wasn't much joy in the air at our house. Were we sad? Disappointed? Not really. Angry or resentful of our circumstances? Not that I remember. We were the four children (three older brothers and me) still at home with my parents after our three oldest sisters had married and were living several states away. We were poor, but I can't honestly remember if I didn't realize it or if it didn't matter. At any rate, it wasn't an issue. If I had to describe what I felt, that's kind of hard because there was no one to blame or be mad at. It was just quiet. I think that's what surprised me most. There was no sound—nobody knew quite what to say, and that's what made it so odd. Nothing was ever quiet around our house, but that Christmas you could have heard a pin drop.

My mother was a saint, and the older I get the more I'm aware of the magic she wove into life. She was never complaining or criticizing; never one to compare our circumstances with those of friends or family members; never less than grateful that God had given us, as it says in 1 Timothy 6:17, ". . . richly all things to enjoy" (NKJV). Maybe she was brainwashing us, but for some reason, whatever the circumstances, they never seemed to bother her; so, consequently, they didn't bother us.

She gave of herself in amazing ways. And she gave not only to us, but seemingly to everyone. The less she had, the more she gave, and the happier she seemed. Jesus himself taught that it's more blessed to give than to receive. I never really doubted that, since I'd seen the genuine demonstration of that truth in the life of my mother. God had given her a job to do, and she did it with a happy heart. If I ever thought about complaining, she'd say convincingly, "Oh, honey, don't think about that now."

Times have changed since the early 1950s when my mother couldn't quite make ends meet. But I'm always reminded that she could put joy in the hearts of her children just by being there for us with a spirit of thanksgiving and joy. She didn't try to be something she wasn't or buy stuff she couldn't. She called upon her Savior to give peace and assurance that he would meet our needs. She was an amazing woman of faith. She encouraged us by her presence and calm. One of the hardest things I've ever tried to do is be objective about my mother. That, to me, would be like being objective about Mother Teresa.

Here's what happened that Christmas. About midday, my uncle Bob—an attorney in a nearby town—showed up unexpectedly with his family. They brought turkey, ham, all the trimmings, and their little sedan full of presents for all. They walked in, announcing that it was boring and lonely at their house (which was, incidentally, huge, warm, brand new, and decorated beautifully for the holidays). They wanted to be with us. And did we ever want to be with them! Many years earlier when my parents were newlyweds, mother had taken this little brother of hers under her wing. She provided nurture and care and somehow was able to help him through law school. He adored my parents, and the feeling was mutual.

God made a way for Uncle Bob through my parents, and now God was making a way for us through him. God can do anything! And in the process he demonstrated great faithfulness to a little girl who, fifty years later, has not forgotten. I can't imagine another Christmas gift that would mean as much to me this long after. It makes me never want to limit God.

When I need encouragement in life, when I'm running on empty and my resources are at their limit, it's easy for me to think of some tangible or physical thing that might meet my need, fill up the emptiness inside, and make me feel whole again. For example, my friends tease me about being a bit of a "purseaholic." When the going gets tough, or when I feel sad and discouraged, I start thinking about purses. It's as if I actually think that if I could just find the perfect purse all my guilt and shame would disappear, my needs would be met, and all would be right with the world. It's such a silly notion, but I'd be lying if I didn't admit I catch those fleeting thoughts meandering through my brain.

Obviously my mother had a much better grip on reality, and her priorities were in better order. My guess is she learned it the hard way. When I was ten months old, my oldest sister died. She was sixteen at the time—a gifted, darling, wonderful girl who was preparing for her senior year of high school. This firstborn and beautiful child had a very special place in my mother's heart, and of course she never recovered from Sybil's death. She vacillated between wondering why she had died and feeling a measure of responsibility about that death. Although Sybil, a healthy teenager, died in the hospital after just two days of severe flulike symptoms, the doctors in those days never considered it a priority to discern the cause of her death. This has always baffled me, and it certainly didn't help my parents cope with the pain, as if any information could have done that anyway. At least it might have freed them from the inevitable guilt.

While Sybil's death had a profound impact on my parents and our whole family the rest of our lives, and while there were many sad, even dreadful aspects of it, God used it in very positive ways. My mother never forgot what real life was all about. It seems her seven remaining children became even more precious to her. Maybe that's why she laid down her life for us. She knew it wasn't so important what was under the tree or on it but who was sitting around it. She knew it didn't matter so much whether or not we were poor but whether or not we were well. She knew the value of our lives was not measured by gifts, regardless of the occasion, and we learned that from her.

To this day, there is a strong, powerful bond between my siblings. As independent as we are, and as spread out geographically, I cannot imagine any circumstance of need in anyone's life when everyone else didn't rally to help. It's something we learned from our mother.

And aren't these the principles God would have us understand? He doesn't want our hearts and minds consumed with *things*. Jesus himself said,

> I say to you, do not worry about your life, what you will eat or what you will drink; nor about your body, what you will put on. Is not life more than food and the body more than clothing? Look at the birds of the air, for they neither sow nor reap nor gather into barns; yet your heavenly Father feeds them. Are you not of more value than they? (Matthew 6:25–26 NKJV)

And our loving one another is of supreme importance to God:

Though I speak with the tongues of men and of angels, but have not love, I have become sounding brass or a clanging cymbal. And though I have the gift of prophecy, and understand all mysteries and all knowledge, and though I have all faith, so that I could remove mountains, but have not love, I am nothing. And though I bestow all my goods to feed the poor, and though I give my body to be burned, but have not love, it profits me nothing. (1 Corinthians 13:1–3 NKJV)

I'm almost sixty now, and most of my life I've been given lavish gifts at Christmas. I've spent hours with friends and family opening so many wonderful presents it takes all day. We even stop for a break or two. And while I love those Christmas mornings, they're not as memorable to me as that cold, damp Christmas in Picher, Oklahoma. That's the one I remember most—when our family came, when the surprise was overwhelming, when my mother was secure and steady about it all, and especially when I learned what's really valuable in life.

⁓   *Holy Father, please accept my humble thanks and praise for your precious Son, whose birth we celebrate at Christmas. We know that he is the greatest gift ever given—wrapped in grace, tied with your heartstrings, and placed on a tree adorned with forgiveness. Thank you, Father. Thank you. Amen.*

Come On, You Can Do It

Barbara Johnson

ᴥ ✳ ᴥ

*Now you are sad, but I will see you again
and you will be happy, and no one will
take away your joy.* (John 16:22 NCV)

My friend Martha was telling me about a little hummingbird that flew into her window. I guess the poor thing thought he would just take a shortcut through the house instead of flying around it, and he ended up with a major headache. In fact, he knocked himself out cold.

Martha thought at first he was dead. He lay spread-eagle on the ground, or I guess you would say spread-hummer. His little wings were stretched out so Martha could see each individual feather, and his tiny green head rested flat on the dirt. She walked slowly out the door toward the little bird, sad to think such a beautiful creature had died in such an unfortunate way. She was just starting to bend down and pick up the corpse so she could give it a decent funeral—or at least sing "Amazing Grace" before she buried it in the flower bed—when something startled her. The bird still lay sprawled out on the ground, unmoving, but suddenly one of those tiny black eyes, no bigger than a pin head, *blinked*.

Martha knelt beside the hummingbird, fascinated as it slowly regained consciousness. The little eye blinked slowly at first, then it slowly gained speed until it almost fluttered. Martha couldn't help herself as the recovery continued. She started talking to the little guy, encouraging him.

"Come on. You can do it," she said. (She told me later she eventually realized she was cooing at the little bird when she should have been humming.)

Slowly, the wings were drawn back in so they lay smoothly against his body.

"Good for you! See? You *can* do it," Martha coaxed.

Next the little head raised groggily off the ground, and soon the threadlike tongue was flickering in and out of the thin, sharp bill.

"Attaboy," Martha cheered. "Keep working at it. You're gonna make it. I just know you will."

It took another minute or two, but soon the hummingbird pulled his feet underneath himself so he was perching on the dirt, and his head began moving left and right, as though he were watching for traffic before crossing the street.

"OK, now. Look how far you've come," Martha said, nearly beside herself with glee. "You just take a big breath and lift those wings, and before you know it . . ."

In an instant the hummer flew away, happily rejoining the crowd at the feeder.

Martha took full credit for his recovery.

"He would never have made it without me there, encouraging him to try," she insisted.

Martha and I have both been on the receiving end of life-restoring encouragement, so we both empathized with that little hummer. We know what it's like to be knocked out cold by life's tricky passages, and we've know what it's like to land spread-eagle on the ground, our head lying in the dirt.

That's why it gave Martha such joy to think she was helping that little hummingbird get back on his feet. To put it into bird-like terms, she knows what it's like to soar again when you think your life has ended. And she knows that the only thing better than soaring yourself is to be the one who helps someone find his wings again when he thinks his flying days are over.

The greatest compliment anyone ever paid me came several years ago when someone called me "the queen of encouragement." I do love to encourage people. Throughout my twenty-some years of writing books and operating Spatula Ministries as an outreach to hurting parents, I've been gratified to receive several nice awards and honors. But none of those things compare with the thrill I get when someone tells me, "Oh, Barb, your books saved my life."

Of course I know that's an exaggeration. The moms who've told me that have had lives that exploded after some tragic setback, and my stories had simply been the spatula that lovingly peeled them off the ceiling. It's not that my writing skills are the best or that my wisdom is any sharper than anyone else's. It's because I'm still here, humming with happiness, even though I've smashed into just about every plateglass window the world has to offer: the death of two sons, the homosexuality of another, being diagnosed with diabetes, the onset of brain cancer, and most recently, the death of my husband.

When you're lying there spread-eagle with your head hanging in the dirt, it's good to have someone come alongside you and say, "I know how you feel. I went through that same head-on collision. I know what it's like when you think your life is over and you're convinced you'll never take another breath, let alone laugh or feel alive with joy. But it happened to me, and it can happen to you. Come on. Get up. You can do it."

In John 16, when Jesus comforted his disciples after telling them he was leaving them, he gave us the perfect example for how to be an encourager. First he acknowledged their feelings, saying, "You will cry and be sad" (v. 20 NCV), and "Now you are sad" (v. 22 NCV).

If you're like me, many times during your life you've been told, "Don't cry," or "Don't be sad." But our emotions are a God-given gift, and sadness is one of the strongest emotions. Tears help cleanse us of our hurt, so it's important to let them flow. That's why, when someone you know has experienced a devastating loss, it's usually better to just go and cry with her rather than worry about saying the right words.

The next part of Jesus's encouragement example in John 16

comes in his reassurance: "Your sadness will become joy" (v. 20 NCV), and "I will see you again and you will be happy, and no one will take away your joy" (v. 22 NCV).

After I went through the death of two sons and the estrangement of another son, who disappeared when we argued about his homosexuality, I spent a year crying and counting the flowers on the wallpaper, completely unable to function. I was at the point of killing myself by driving off a viaduct when my heart—and my car—made a U-turn. I gave my troubled mind—and my homosexual son—to God and said, "Whatever, Lord!" And that's when the most amazing thing happened. It was as though a million little sparkles started building inside me, and soon an incomprehensible bubble of joy pushed all the sadness out of my heart and a peace that passes all understanding filled my life.

Just as Jesus told his disciples what would happen as they believed in him, my sadness became joy, too, and despite all that I've been through and knowing that other difficulties may lie ahead, I'm convinced no one can ever take that joy away from me.

Sure, there's still sadness in my life. Sure, I sometimes think I cannot endure one more setback. But then I remember Jesus's words, and I remember my own experiences, how his promise has worked within me in the past. And then I know I can endure any difficulties, remembering there is relief on the other side of them—and believing my sadness will turn to joy.

Then it's on to the next step: sharing the blessing. What a wonderful thing it is to be the one who weeps with that freshly hurting mother but also, when the timing is right, shares Jesus's words to reassure her that she'll survive the heartache: *Now you are sad, but . . . you will be happy, and no one will take away your joy.*

Seeing those ancient words printed on the page is one thing, but seeing them lived out *today* is another. It's something so powerful it can turn sadness to joy. That's why it's so important for us plateglass-window veterans to keep coaxing and reassuring the more recent crashers until their heads clear, their eyes can see again, and they finally understand the truth of what we're saying: "Jesus did it for me, and he can do it for you too."

ᔥ *Dear Jesus, your Word encourages me when I've crashed into yet another barrier. Thank you for lifting me up when I've fallen to the ground. Thank you for helping my spirit soar again when I've lost my wings of hope. You are my Healer and my Comforter. Amen.*

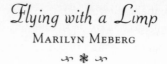

Flying with a Limp

MARILYN MEBERG

ა✱ა

God deliberately chose things the world considers foolish in order to shame those who think they are wise. (1 CORINTHIANS 1:27 NLT)

*H*ave you ever seen a bird fly with a limp? I'm not talking about limping about on the patio. I'm talking about limping about in the air.

I was working out on my treadmill. (I'm trying to lower my cholesterol without resorting to pills. Most days I say "What's wrong with taking a pill? It's quick, painless, and not boring. But then the crabby voice starts up in my head, so I sigh and keep treading.) The reason my treadmill figures into all this is that its location upstairs is next to a huge window. The scene from the window serves to remind me how much I'm loving my new home state of Texas. From my above-the-roofline perch I can see a gazillion recently "hatched" flowers, vibrantly green, new-leafed trees, and birds. But I'd never seen a flying limp before.

Most birds manage gliding, effortless swoops and turns which have always inspired my envy. Since childhood I've wanted to fly as a bird does. But in this case, I felt no envy, only curiosity and basic disbelief. What in the world was this bird doing with its wings that caused it to look handicapped? It appeared capable of dropping to earth in one quick lurch. What really threw me is that the winged limper is a cardinal. Cardinals knock me out with their dramatic scarlet-and-black throat and face. This one appeared to be recovering from a knock-out of its own.

Naturally I assumed it had been injured. Keeping my eye on him, I noticed no limping when he walked and did whatever aimless things birds do on the ground, but as soon as he took to the air, his erratic up and down surges went into effect again.

I asked myself if I would feel the same level of disbelief if the bird had not been a Cardinal. If it had been a drab little starling, would I have felt general compassion but not disbelief? I guess there is something about external beauty and perfection that is startled when that beauty is visibly altered. Cardinals are supposed to look as gorgeous when they fly as they do perching regally on my patio chair. This one didn't live up to its cardinal standard of excellence.

I reminded myself that there's a little something wrong with everything and everyone in life. That's why I was on the treadmill. I looked at my gorgeous limper sitting exquisitely on a tree branch and felt a soft kinship. I guess neither one of us was in the best of conditions.

Though there is a little something wrong with life and wrong with us, there's a lot that's right as well. One of the most "right with life" experiences I enjoy is friendship. But the reality is, all my friends have little limps in their souls. They don't do things perfectly. They don't always fly straight. Sometimes they even *lunge* through their day. I love that about them because I have so many limping imperfections; these limping friends are perfect for me. Ralph Waldo Emerson said one of the blessings of friends is that you can afford to be stupid with them. I suppose we could change Emerson's wording to "You can afford to limp with them."

One of my recent stupid limps, which Luci Swindoll experienced, was my generous offer to pick up a few groceries for her. I was heading out for food reinforcements and offered to pick up a few things for her. She gave me a list.

Forty minutes later I knocked on her door with her bag of items. As I spread them out on her counter, we both became quiet and simply stared. There were two packages of Twinkies, two cans of Ajax, one bottle of mouthwash guaranteed to remove plaque, an easy-pour bottle of Lysol deodorizing cleaner that cuts grease and disinfects, and an eight-ounce can of Bud Lite.

Her response to this bewildering array of items, which I did not remember picking out, putting in my basket, or paying for was, "Marilyn, the only thing I can use here is the can of Bud Lite" (she was kidding, of course).

"Well, but I have no idea where this stuff came from. I must have scooped someone else's items up and left them with mine.

Someone in Frisco is going to open their bag and find vanilla yogurt, white cheddar cheese, unsalted wheat thin crackers, and a package of Hefty garbage bags."

After a thoughtful silence Luci said, " What about my eggs?"

"You didn't have eggs on your list."

"No, and I didn't have Bud Lite on there either!"

It would be fun to tell you about the times some of us Women of Faith speakers missed our flight departures because we misread our tickets, or left a jacket wadded on the plane seat next to us, or mistakenly put a restaurant spoon in "our" purse to be discovered later when searching for the evening niacin pills.

"How did the spoon get in the purse?"

"Beats me."

"Me, too."

How could my friends and I misread a flight schedule, leave a jacket wadded in seat B on American flight 2021, buy Bud Lite instead of eggs, or stick a spoon in our purse, which belongs to Texas Land and Cattle restaurant? These are the limpings of the well-intended and misinformed, but I am endlessly and joyfully encouraged by it all.

It seems to me that God has a special place for those creatures and persons who cannot live up to the cardinal standard of excellence. Read this great passage from 1 Corinthians 1:26–29 and see if you too don't feel better about your occasional limps:

Remember, dear brothers and sisters, that few of you were wise in the world's eyes, or powerful, or wealthy when God called you. Instead, God deliberately chose things the world considers foolish in order to shame those who think they are wise. And he chose those who are powerless to shame those who are powerful. God chose things despised by the world, things counted as nothing at all, and used them to bring to nothing what the world considers important, so that no one can ever boast in the presence of God. (NLT)

❧   *Father God, thank you for being patient with me as I limp along through life, making mistakes and living well intentioned, but below your standard of excellence. Thank you for lifting me up and encouraging me each time I fall. Amen.*

PART 8

❧

Joy Applauds

Exuberant with Applause
BARBARA JOHNSON
ꜱ ✳ ꜱ

So you'll go out in joy, you'll be led into a whole and complete life.
The mountains and hills will lead the parade, bursting with song. All
the trees of the forest will join the procession, exuberant with
applause. (ISAIAH 55:12 MSG)

*E*veryone loves applause, but when I was traveling with
Women of Faith, applause was sometimes a mixed blessing. All
the participants must keep to a strict schedule, and a little clock
on the side of the stage counts down the time remaining as each
woman gives her presentation. Frankly, I had so much to say and
so little time to say it, sometimes I would smile and flutter my
hands if the audience interrupted me with applause and say,
"Oh, no. Don't clap. I don't have time for that!"

It probably seemed a little ungrateful of me, although I certainly didn't intend it that way. Now that I've stepped out of the
spotlight to deal with my brain cancer, I occasionally think it
would be nice to hear that appreciative applause again.
Everyone needs a good dose of praise now and then.

I've heard so many heartwarming stories that describe the power that praise and applause can have. I get teary-eyed every time I watch a TV news story about a group of soldiers, sailors, or marines being deployed into a war zone and having their families and friends there with flags and banners, cheering and applauding to send their loved ones off with proud and loving praise ringing in their ears.

Or consider the different types of applause you might hear at the various marathons that are held around the country. The televised images of the winner crossing the finish line in front of grandstands filled with cheering fans aren't as meaningful to me as the pictures of those others, far back in the pack, who are so exhausted they seem to be struggling simply to put one foot in front of the other. But then they turn a corner or top a hill, and there's their family or friends, cheering for them, clapping their hands and calling out encouragement, and suddenly the runner's grimace is replaced by a grin, and the pounding sneakers seem to go just a little faster.

By the time some of these slow-but-determined marathoners reach the finish line, the grandstands are being removed and the crowds have gone home. But there's that little cheering section again, whooping it up as though their runner had just won an Olympic gold medal. Sometimes the runner will tell an interviewer later, "I didn't think I could make it. I was ready to give up. Then I heard my husband's voice, cheering for me, and my son clapping and saying, 'Go, Mom, go!' I don't know what happened, exactly, but I got this little surge of energy, and it helped me keep going."

How fabulous the power of applause can be—and not just for the recipient of the applause but for the applauders too.

When wildfires plagued southwest Colorado a few years ago, an army of firefighters flooded the area, setting up tent cities in hot, dry parking lots, and heading out into the high-altitude, ninety-degree heat every day to fight the fires that raged throughout the area, destroying many homes and devastating the beautiful scenery. A friend who has a summer home there told me that throughout the area, residents posted signs on their mailboxes and hung bedsheets spray-painted with messages of gratitude to the men and women who had come to stand between them and the raging inferno. "You could hardly drive a mile through the countryside without seeing some kind of sign that said, 'Thank you, firefighters!'" the woman said.

She and her family attended an outdoor music program at a chuck-wagon barbecue place less than two weeks after it had been saved by the firefighters. To get there, they drove through a ghostly forest of charred pines and ash-covered ground, but the quaint, old gathering place itself had been spared, thanks to the heroic efforts of the firefighters.

The woman and her family joined a large crowd that had come to celebrate the landmark business's survival, and as they were finding their table, she heard a single pair of hands start clapping. Then other hands joined in. The woman turned to see what had sparked the applause and saw a line of firefighters, all dressed in their bright yellow shirts and olive green cargo pants, slowly filing in to find their table as well. The owner of the eating place had extended an open invitation to any of them who were hungry, and about twenty of them were there that night. By the time they had settled onto the benches alongside their picnic tables, all the diners—and even the cooks and servers—were on their feet, applauding loudly and cheering wildly.

The firefighters smiled in embarrassment, nodding their heads and lifting their hands shyly to acknowledge the applause. It was a special moment for everyone there, the woman told me, and more than one person was wiping away tears. The firefighters obviously felt gratified by the residents' exuberant thanks, and the residents were delighted to have a chance to express it to them one on one.

That's the thing about applause and praise. It can be as good for the giver as it is for the recipient.

And, like joy, applause can be wonderfully contagious. More than ten years ago, I saved this little story from a book edited by Arthur F. Lenehan called *The Best of Bits & Pieces* (published by Economics Press in Fairfield, New Jersey) that shows what an important message applause can carry—and how contagious applause and acclamation can be.

A sold-out crowd had gathered in the concert hall to hear a world-famous singer perform. But before the program began, this announcement brought a groan from the crowd: "Ladies and gentlemen, we apologize for any disappointment this announcement may cause. Our featured singer has suffered a minor accident and will be unable to perform tonight. We hope you will welcome his understudy warmly."

The substitute singer gave it his all, but not once was his performance interrupted by applause. Even at the end of the opera, his contribution went unacknowledged by the crowd—until the voice of a little girl rang out from the balcony, exclaiming, "Daddy, I think you were wonderful!"

Suddenly, as though reminded of their manners, the audience members joined the child in her acclaim, and the concert hall erupted into thunderous applause.

One way or another, we all need some applause and praise in our lives. And guess what: so does God. Again and again, the Bible tells us to praise our Creator. Read the Psalms, and you'll see that we're to praise God with song, with dancing, with tambourines and harps, with trumpet blasts and loud cymbals—and I'm sure he wouldn't mind a little applause now and then either.

The Bible tells us it's not just us humans who are to shower God with praise. All creation—sun and moon, shining stars, angels and armies, heaven and earth, "the seas and everything in them" (Psalm 69:34 NCV)—should praise him. We're to praise him because he is holy and wonderful and great, and we're to praise him for his kindness and goodness and for everything he has done for us. God wants us to praise him!

So much of the time our prayers are only pleas for help. God welcomes those needy prayers, but just as any parent gets tired of hearing, "Please, please, please!" so does God. And of course we know to thank God for all the blessings he has bestowed on us. He likes to hear our words of gratitude as well. But the thing most of us probably forget to do is simply to praise him—to say, "Yea, God!" now and then to cheer him on and let him know we admire him and respect him.

After all, God made us in his image, and since we like to hear applause, that must mean he does too! When's the last time you prayed *simply to praise God?* Don't wait any longer. Do it right now in words, in songs, and even in dancing. (Just a thought—some of us might want to do this in a private place.)

~ *Glorious God, Creator of heaven and earth, we praise you for your holiness, your majesty, your greatness, and your magnificent power. We praise you with our hearts, souls, and minds. We praise you for your kindness and goodness and for everything you have done for us. You are our awesome Father, our sovereign King, and our all-powerful Protector. Glory be to you, O God most high! Amen.*

Reading Between the Lines
LUCI SWINDOLL

ᵔ ✳ ᵔ

As cold water to a weary soul, so is good news from a far country.
(PROVERBS 25:25 NKJV)

*N*ot long ago, I received a greeting card that made me glad
to be alive, not just because it came from somebody I love and
treasure, but because the card itself is a work of art. On the front
there's a photograph of a Lithuanian woman enthusiastically
greeting her dog. She's reaching down to kiss the dog just as he
is reaching up to receive her kiss. Both figures are overweight,
unkempt, past their prime, and as happy as can be. It's a magnificent photo I wish I had taken. Just above that photo is a typed
sentence that reads, "Those who make us happy deserve our
thanks." That line alone is worth the price of the card. I had a
hard time figuring out which I loved more—the picture or the
inscription.

Including the sweet handwritten note from my friend, I

found everything about the card endearing, even the commercial information on the back. A small paragraph explained that the photo is from the M.I.L.K. collection—"Moments of intimacy, laughter, and kinship." It's one of three hundred (out of forty thousand) diverse entries worldwide that captures the essence of humanity, based on the belief that people should be celebrated. That's what it says in a small space. I read it over and over again because I liked it so much.

Somebody took time out of a busy life to dream up the idea of gathering pictures that cut across race, nationality, and status, to show us what it means to be part of a family, to share the gift of friendship, and most of all, to be loved. I grew up in a family of communicators. The shelves in my garage are filled with boxes of correspondence from members of my immediate and extended family. Those handwritten notes, photos, scraps of paper, dog-eared letters, and pieces of mail attest to the ways my family loved to visit with one another.

I've saved many of the postcards my father's brother wrote his mom during World War I when he was stationed in France. Each tells a little story of his activities and homesickness for the family he left behind. One I especially like reads, "This picture shows a machine gun used to guard the camps on the border. They are playing a big part on the Front Line now."

And get this: my grandmother wrote letters to us on small lined paper, but when those lines were filled with information she thought important, that didn't stop her from continuing to write. She scribbled more notes in all the margins. When we had finished reading her letters, they had been turned upside down and over many times. She must have invented the phrase "reading between the lines."

When I was a college student, my parents wrote me letters regularly. Mother reported on the neighborhood—who had done what, who was ill or had just gotten well, who had bought a new car or gotten a new pet, who was being prayed for on our street and why. Daddy wrote love notes full of little drawings, poetry, Scripture references, and great quotations to live by. Together, Mother and Daddy applauded me with intimacy and laughter from their daily life and made me feel a close kinship when I was miles away. Between them, I was kept well informed and cherished. Those letters were better than phone calls, because I could hold them in my hands and read them again and again.

Those days are a distant memory now, but love, joy, and relationship still encourage me in wonderful and meaningful ways today through e-mails from my brothers and dear friends. Some of them report the details of daily life, and others send words of wisdom and counsel. I look forward to the joy that comes with both.

Recently, I was in England on vacation and received several e-mails from my close, sweet friend, Ney Bailey. Ney has traveled the world and seen many more miles of foreign roads than I, but this time she was the one who stayed home. I absolutely loved her e-mails. They were full of news and updates about our neighborhood—who's buying what house, the landscape work taking place in the yard next to mine, what's going on at church while I'm gone. And because Ney has walked with the Lord for more than fifty years, those notes were replete with Scripture, tenderness, encouragement, and quotes from the great books she was reading. My e-mails back to her often felt like paltry attempts at just keeping her informed, but she assured me she was happy when they came, so I stayed at it in spite of feelings of inadequacy at times. As the Bible says, "As cold water to a weary soul, so is good news from a far country" (Proverbs 25:25 NKJV).

As much as I cherish personal mail from my family and friends; as much as it gives me interesting information and reminds me how loved I am; as much as my soul is encouraged by all these examples of communication, there are letters written to me that surpass all of these. And those same letters are written to you. They are filled with information and the greatest intimacy the world has ever known.

When Jesus lived on this planet, he communicated in life-changing ways. He talked with children, ate with friends, encountered men and women on their way to work, always showing them love and kindness in their humanity, no matter their race, nationality, or status. Although nobody had a camera back then to capture all this milk of human kindness on a greeting card, Jesus's disciples recorded the depth of Jesus's love notes in letters and journals. These make up the first four books of the New Testament. Daily, Jesus demonstrated through word pictures the importance of warm communication. Sometimes it was "neighborhood news" of his life and times the disciples wrote, and sometimes it was instruction for life. We often read passages that remind us how loved and cherished we are by the Shepherd of our souls.

As a child, I grew up knowing there was nothing ever written or said as important as the Word of God. If no one ever sent me another e-mail, postcard, or letter, I have his Word to bring joy to my soul.

Last year at a Women of Faith conference in Oklahoma City, I was reminded of just how long the Bible has been my most important source of comfort and instruction. A woman I didn't know walked up to where I was signing books. She was holding a very old, worn Bible that had my name engraved on the front. Wordlessly, she laid it down and waited for my response. I didn't recognize it at first, but after a few minutes of staring at it, I said, "That's my name, but how do you happen to have this Bible?"

She told me I had given it to her mother fifty years ago, but her mom wanted to return it "so it can mentor someone else." She explained that she was seven years old when her mother got it, and that it had been a tremendous comfort to both of them all these years.

"My mother now lives in a nursing facility and is eighty-two," she said. "But she asked me to bring it to you this weekend with her appreciation for all the years she's enjoyed it."

I recognized that old Bible from my youth, full of my underlining, markings, and margin study notes. I remember how in college I had been an enthusiastic student of God's Word; so when my friend commented on liking that Bible, I gave it to her. Now, at the age of seventy-two, it had come back to me not only as a complete surprise but a source of joy.

Nothing is more important than words. In fact, my favorite

invention on earth is the alphabet. Where would we be without it? Don't hesitate to say words that build up and strengthen someone. Applaud others with kind words. And put them in writing to be kept and cherished (otherwise, the shelves in their garages will be empty.) And read often the words God has spoken to you, personally. Study the Scriptures, memorize them, feed on them like the bread of life. They will nourish your soul. Remember the words of Job in chapter 23, verse 12: "I have not departed from the commandment of His lips; I have treasured the words of His mouth more than my necessary food" (NKJV).

If you want to make someone happy, figure out how to say thank you in a fresh, loving way. Send a card. Write a warm, tender e-mail. Communicate the good news instead of the bad. Mail a postcard or a letter. Send someone you love a detailed description of everything going on in the neighborhood. Tell them what you love and miss about them. Celebrate someone! Give them a Bible—one you won't need for another fifty years.

✺ *Father, I cherish the letters you have written to me. I love the beautiful stories and messages of grace revealed in your Word. And I treasure my dog-eared copy that reminds me of the many intimate hours we've spent together. Thanks for writing, Dad. Amen.*

Say It Loud and Clear!

SHEILA WALSH

ى ✳ ى

Whoever has the gift of encouraging others should encourage.
(ROMANS 12:8 NCV)

*E*ach one of us has a body with many parts, and these parts all have different uses. In the same way, we are many, but in Christ we are all one body. Each one is a part of that body, and each part belongs to all the other parts. We all have different gifts, each of which came because of the grace God gave us. The person who has the gift of prophecy should use that gift in agreement with the faith. Anyone who has the gift of serving should serve. Anyone who has the gift of teaching should teach. Whoever has the gift of encouraging others should encourage. Whoever has the gift of giving to others should give freely. Anyone who has the gift of being a leader should try hard when he leads. Whoever has the gift of showing mercy to others should do so with joy. (Romans 12:4–8 NCV)

I am not usually at a loss for words, but recently I had an experience that left me completely speechless. I was invited to speak at the Master's Commission's annual conference in Phoenix, Arizona. For those of you who are new to Master's Commission, it's a hands-on discipleship training program especially for teens. Young people commit at least a year of their lives in learning how to serve our Master. Their call is to a lifestyle of total commitment to Christ with an emphasis on prayer, the Word of God, evangelism, and servanthood. Once a year they gather for an international conference to inspire, challenge, and motivate one another to a deeper walk with Christ.

I didn't know much about the ministry, but as the conference was being held at First Assembly, Phoenix, pastor Tommy Barnett's church, I knew it would be a very worthwhile experience. I just had no idea what was in store or how it would impact my life.

It all started like this. As I was leaving my house in Texas on Thursday morning to catch my flight, I saw two boxes on the doorstep addressed to Barry and Christian. I didn't realize then that this was just the beginning of an outpouring of love and grace on our lives. When Barry opened the boxes he discovered that the leaders in Phoenix wanted to bless my family while I was gone. As they unpacked their gifts, they found a fishing rod and reel for Christian and a huge bucket of fresh-boiled peanuts from South Carolina for Barry—perfect gifts! They were overwhelmed that even though they were not physically with me, they had been included in the celebration.

I landed in Phoenix and was met by a darling girl who took me to the church to do a sound check. Then I was taken to the hotel to prepare for that evening. In my room was a gift basket full of fruit, cookies, teas, and bottled water. A beautiful bouquet of fresh flowers sat by my nightstand. I had a quick shower and changed for the evening and then went back to the church.

We prayed together as a team, and then I spent a little time with Rev. Lloyd Zeigler, a remarkable man and the director of Master's Commission. He talked about his passionate commitment to our young people, to help them find God's vision and direction for their lives. Then I followed him into a packed auditorium.

Boy, did I feel old! There was a rap group onstage that was tearing the house down! Christian would have been in his element. I watched the young people dancing at the front with radiant faces and uplifted hands. When the worship team took the stage, I was struck by the authenticity of their worship. They had written all their own songs, and there was a flavor that's missing from some of our corporate worship in the evangelical church. They sang out all their emotions. They sang out their fear and their struggles as well as their hope and praise. It reminded me of the psalmist David, who wrote from the deepest recesses of his soul and spirit.

Before I spoke, I was invited to come up on stage and sit in a chair. I wasn't quite sure what was going to happen. Lloyd told me that each of the different chapters wanted to honor God's work through my life. As I sat there, young men and women knelt at my feet and brought gifts that they had carefully chosen to express their hearts. One group said, "One of the things that we love most is how much you love your son, so our gifts are for him." Some brought journals, knowing that I love to take notes. Others brought candles, one a C. S. Lewis devotional. Each gift seemed more meaningful than the one before. One young girl put a box at my feet, and when I opened it, inside lay Dorothy from the *Wizard of Oz*, reminding me that I am not home yet. A young man placed a large bell before me, explaining that this was a Navy SEAL bell. It was only later when I read the note that I understood the significance.

When one of the highly trained military elite known as the Navy SEALs feels that he can no longer carry on, he rings a bell. It is a sad sound for them that means one of their comrades has given up. As I looked at my bell, I realized that they had removed the clapper and taped a note inside that said, "Never give up!" I wept through the whole experience. I have never felt so humbled and blessed in my entire life. What made it even more overwhelming was that when I wasn't feeling at all well and at my most vulnerable I was showered with love and grace. What a gift! What an amazing surprise from God as he blessed me and renewed me in a way I didn't even expect.

When it was time for me to speak, the young people stood and applauded for a long time. I was very touched by that. We live in a culture that is used to the sight of a standing ovation at the end of a performance, but what happened to me that night had nothing to do with that. What I experienced was the encouragement and love of the body of Christ based on nothing that I might bring to them that night but based on their heartfelt desire to honor a sister in Christ. That beautiful thread ran through the entire conference. No matter who was taking part or what gift they had to offer, they were received with joy and grace.

Can you imagine how that would impact our families and churches if we received each other in this way? If someone has a wonderful singing voice or can muster up a pretty decent sermon, then we will applaud and encourage, but we are all the body of Christ. Each one of us brings the gifts we have been given, and the more we are welcomed in that gift, the more we flourish.

Even as I write I think of all of you who serve God faithfully and yet never have a moment when those around you stop and say, "Thank you!" Perhaps you are never able to make it to an event where thousands of women worship together, but there is One who misses nothing. Your heavenly Father sees everything you do, every sacrifice you make, every selfless choice, and he rejoices over you.

Beloved, let us love: love is of God;
In God alone hath love its true abode.
Beloved, let us love: for they who love,
they only, are His sons, born from above.
Beloved, let us love: for love is rest,
and he who loveth not abides unblest.
Beloved, let us love: for love is light,
and he who loveth not dwelleth in night.

Beloved, let us love: for only thus
shall we behold that God Who loveth us.
—HORATIUS BONAR

May you know God's loving gaze this day in all you do, and may we choose to live a life of great appreciation for the gifts that God has placed in each one of his children. And may we say it loud and clear!

ↄ *Dear Father, I want to use my life to honor and applaud you as you have done for me. Receive my gift of praise and adoration in love. And please help me to instill a heart of joy and praise in others through the name of Jesus. Amen.*

Remembering Grace

MARY GRAHAM

⊱ ✳ ⊰

For by grace you have been saved . . . it is the gift of God.
(EPHESIANS 2:8 NKJV)

$\mathcal{I}$t's been one of the great privileges of my life to sit under the Bible teaching of Chuck Swindoll since the late 1970s. When I first met his sister, Luci, I'd never heard of him. He was just beginning to be heard nationwide on the radio, and his first book had just been published. (The church where he was pastor in Southern California was already packed every Sunday, for *five* services! And I remember Luci saying how early we'd have to go to church. I said, "Who *is* your brother?" It seemed unbelievable that we had to go so early just to ensure we'd have a place to sit. It's not like we were going to a concert or football game!)

Since then, Chuck has influenced my life profoundly. His understanding of the grace of God is unparalleled, and that perspective comes through again and again in his sermons and in his writings. In recent weeks I've been listening again to his The Grace Awakening series. It was first taught in the 1980s but is as fresh and relevant today as if it had just been written. I'm loving this fresh reminder of who God is and how he works.

Needing to move to Texas a few years ago, I made it a point to live in a neighborhood close to the church where he currently ministers. Understanding and being reminded of God's grace is, for me, an essential need of life, like eating and drinking.

It changes me a tiny measure every time I remember the Christian life is not about what I do; it's about what he does for me. Holding on to that reality brings such a magic to life day by day.

At the Women of Faith conference in St. Paul in 2004, our lighting crew chief, Pete Malvezzi, suffered a severe double brain aneurysm. It all happened so suddenly. After the evening session on Friday, several members of the crew and I gathered around a table in catering as we always do for the technical briefing for the day on Saturday. We waited for a while for Pete and Scott, the production manager, to join us. As it got later, I began to inquire about what was detaining them. That's when I learned that Pete had had a massive headache toward the end of the evening, had collapsed on the production manager's office floor, and the EMT professionals had been summoned. They raced him to the hospital, and the entire crew followed.

It wasn't until the wee hours of the next morning when Amy, one of the staff on the Women of Faith leadership team, phoned me in the hotel with the horrific news. The doctors gave us no hope for his survival.

Amy said, "Mary, it's horrible. I've been here in the hospital all night, and the crew guys were all going into intensive care one by one to say good-bye to Pete. They were sobbing, and it was so sad, Mary. It was so sad."

I'd never heard Amy so broken. The story unfolded. "The doctor put him on life support until his wife and mom could get here. They're coming in a couple of hours, and I'll pick them up at the airport. I didn't want to tell you during the night because I knew you and the speakers needed your rest for the conference today."

Throughout that Saturday, as we walked through the minutes of the conference with our extremely responsive audience, God gave us such grace to minister to others in spite of our broken hearts. The team on the platform and the entire team behind the scenes were overwhelmed with sadness all day. During the breaks we slipped backstage to cry and pray and make quick little trips to the nearby hospital to see Pete, his wife, and his mom. We all knew we were saying good-bye to him that day. Only God's grace sustained us. We had no strength or courage of our own.

It seemed important at the time to not share the story with the audience. They were there for a day of personal refreshment and certainly were bearing burdens of their own. We wanted them to have their Women of Faith day, and we knew Pete would have wanted us to think only of the audience. (We later learned, however, that our very sensitive audience of women had been observing us all day and wondering if something might be wrong.)

When Sheila prepared to close the conference with prayer

on Saturday, she brought the audience into our sorrow, explained our burden, and asked the eighteen thousand women to pray for Pete. When she did, she mentioned that some in the audience might have some loved one who was also, at that moment, in a life-threatening situation. She asked that those women stand as a representative of their loved one when she prayed for our Pete. To our amazement, hundreds stood all over the arena. It was one of those moments none of us will ever forget. And at that very moment, two blocks away in an intensive care hospital room, Pete's condition began to change. The nurses, we later learned, were shaking their heads and wondering why he was beginning to show small signs of response. From that moment, he made steady progress toward complete restoration. The next day, the exceedingly baffled brain specialists looked at him with disbelief and said to someone on our staff, "You guys must have *some* connection to heaven."

That all happened in October 2004. By the end of May 2005, Pete was able to visit a Women of Faith conference near his home with his wife and small son. By the early part of July, he was back at his post commandeering an exceedingly complicated lighting board that has an array of formidable switches, knobs, handles, and complex connections. I walk by him every weekend now and see him pushing and pulling levers and knowing exactly what to do. Still quiet and somewhat shy, he always looks up now and we exchange knowing smiles. Our whole team—staff, speakers, guests, and crew—know something no one in the audience knows. We know that once in our lives we held hands, cried, prayed, and together saw a miracle—our own personal miracle.

I cannot get over what happened. I'm not necessarily one who believes we see such dramatic, implausible, unbelievable miracles every day. Silly me. I have no words, except *grace*. God does great work when we can do nothing. He thrives on the impossible. None of us deserve it, nor have earned it, nor have anything to do with it. He sheds his grace all over our lives. He engages us in his mission of love for all mankind, and he performs miracles in and through us. We don't always see what he does on our behalf, but he's always at work by his power and his grace. I learned that from Chuck Swindoll, but I've rarely seen it so dramatically played out as in the life and "death" and life of Pete Malvezzi.

Why would God do that? We'll never know fully perhaps, but we see so much that was accomplished through this drama. Many came to faith in Christ for the first time. Many understood the incredible power of our prayers. Many were encouraged that we are not alone—in the face of the unthinkable, God can do the impossible. The passage in Ephesians 2 says it all:

> But God, who is rich in mercy, because of His great love with which He loved us, even when we were dead in trespasses, made us alive together with Christ (by grace you have been saved), and raised us up together, and made us sit together in the heavenly places in Christ Jesus, that in the ages to come He might show the

exceeding riches of His grace in His kindness toward us in Christ Jesus. For by grace you have been saved through faith, and that not of yourselves; it is the gift of God. (vv. 4–8 NKJV)

It's amazing how easily we can slip into thinking that it's about us—what *we* do or don't; what *we* think or don't, who *we* are or aren't, instead of remembering it's all about *him* and *his* grace. And he plans to show us the exceeding riches of his grace *in kindness toward us*. My guess is that most of us go through a lot of days and weeks and months without giving a single thought to that. Instead, it's easy to think about ourselves and wonder, *Oh, boy. What did I not do now that I should have done?* We forget it's all grace—his grace *to* us, and flowing *through* us, and *changing* us from within.

It makes me tremble that I could ever forget his grace, the power of prayer, and the part we are entrusted to play in his purposes on this earth.

Pete's illness and recovery have left an indelible mark on Women of Faith.

~ *O Lord, how can I even begin to say thanks for your incredible grace and mercy? I'm overwhelmed with joy and gratitude every time I remember what you've done for me. With every breath, O God, I praise and glorify your holy name. Amen.*

A Standing Ovation for God

NICOLE JOHNSON

ᷤ ❋ ᷤ

Shout for joy, O heavens; rejoice, O earth!
(ISAIAH 49:13 NIV)

*J*oy is the heart's way of applauding. That wonderful feeling that rises up inside that we call joy is the heart clapping wildly. If the hands can clap when the heart is not in it, why can't the heart clap without involving the hands? I don't mean to start a war between body parts, but isn't the heart's applause and approval even deeper than what involves mere hand clapping or whistling? Joy is the deep sense of the heart's full accordance and approval over something that brings it deep satisfaction and happiness. When the heart chooses to applaud alone, the result is the lifting of our spirit in joy.

Whenever I think about joy as a state of the heart, the words to the hymn "Joyful, Joyful, We Adore Thee" just spring to my mind, and the tune immediately plays across my heart. It is such a lifting, happy, joyous response to God, and my heart instantly begins to clap. It is one of my favorite hymns to sing in church, and whenever it's selected it elevates my spirit and creates joy. Sometimes this song makes a good morning even better, and sometimes it turns a less than biblical mood into something vaguely recognizable in the New Testament.

When the music starts, and my mouth forms the first few words, that's when joy, my heart's applause, rises up taking my spirit and mood along with it. It's almost impossible to sing these lyrics with a frown on your face, a wrinkle in your soul, or a worry in your heart. Not that I haven't seen people do it, but for me, it relaxes that furrow in my brow, smoothes some of the disheveled places in my soul, and comforts the concerns of my heart.

Can't you just feel the author's heart lifting and face beaming as he wrote these words?

Joyful, joyful, we adore Thee, God of glory, Lord of love:
Hearts unfold like flowers before Thee, opening to the sun
above.
Melt the clouds of sin and sadness; drive the dark of
doubt away;
Giver of immortal gladness, fill us with the light of day!

Henry Jackson van Dyke wrote the words to this incredible hymn in 1907. He was a pastor and later became a professor of English literature at Princeton. He was in western Massachusetts speaking at Williams College when he penned the words.

Apparently the Berkshires were his inspiration, and the lines just flowed from him one morning while he was staying in the home of the president of the college, Harry Garfield. When van Dyke presented the lyrics to Garfield before he was to speak at the college that very morning, he told Harry that it must be sung to the tune of Beethoven's "Hymn to Joy."

I would like to visit the Berkshires and see what he was seeing when he wrote his verses. It must have been so inspiring. Maybe he awoke in the morning after an unusually good night's sleep and stretched his arms and his heart to take in the wonderful fresh mountain air. Perhaps he stood on a little balcony or deck and heard the birds singing, or a brook running over the rocks down below him, and joy just rose up like applause in his heart. I wonder if he penned this verse just based on what he was seeing around him, because the words seem so much about his *view*. As his heart applauded with joy, he wrote this verse:

> All Thy works with joy surround Thee, earth and heav'n
> reflect Thy rays,
> Stars and angels sing around Thee, center of unbroken
> praise;
> Field and forest, vale and mountain, flowery meadow,
> flashing sea,
> Chanting bird and flowing fountain call us to rejoice in Thee.

To whom do most people attribute beauty in the world? Many never think about it. A person of faith has the Creator to thank for life's good gifts, but too often we don't say thank you or allow our hearts to applaud sheer beauty. G. K. Chesterton came to believe in God because he needed a place to put his gratitude. He wanted someone to thank for the goodness and beauty of the earth. He remarked once at Christmas that his children had him to thank for putting good things in their stockings, but "have I no one to thank for putting two feet in mine?" Overflowing gratitude called him not only to believe, but to rejoice in having a Creator.

> Thou art giving and forgiving, ever blessing, ever blessed,
> Wellspring of the joy of living, ocean-depth of happy rest!
> Thou our Father, Christ our Brother, all who live in love
>   are Thine;
> Teach us how to love each other, lift us to the joy divine.

If you have ever wondered where you might find more joy, take a look at that second line again. The author calls God the "wellspring of the joy of living." A wellspring is a plentiful source or supply—a fountainhead that just gushes refreshing, clean water. God, in his lavish love and forgiveness, is the origin and supplier of the joy of living. God is a wellspring that runs underneath our lives; he's an underground spring that feeds us with the joy of being alive, as our hearts are watered by him. Then we begin to splash in his love and forgiveness, and we learn to love and forgive each other. We are carried along in this magnificent stream, and taken to the ultimate place—divine joy.

The words of this hymn exude the kind of confidence that marks truth. The bold assertion of these lyrics is that for those who know God, the heart's response is joy. Because of his love, we love, and our lives are full of blessing and peace. And then comes this invitation:

> Mortals, join the happy chorus, which the morning stars began;
> Father love is reigning o'er us, brother love binds man to man.
> Ever singing, march we onward, victors in the midst of strife;
> Joyful music leads us sunward in the triumph song of life.

Come on, mortals, add your voice to the song that the stars began long ago. You don't have to carry the tune; just join the chorus. Join the happy chorus made up of morning stars that know the goodness of God and perhaps even know the end of history—and they are happy! It all turns out OK. The stars are rejoicing and applauding because the Father of all love is on the throne of the universe, and what a reason to celebrate.

And what a choir to celebrate with! I've sung with a group or two in my life, but definitely not a choir like this one. How can we resist the invitation to sing and march onward, knowing that it gives us victory in the midst of strife? Everyone I know is looking for that—who knew that we just needed to join this choir to find it? This joyful music, this applause of the heart, is what lifts us up toward the light of all life. Later in life, commenting on the lyrics, Jackson van Dyke said,

These verses are simple expressions of common

Christian feelings and desires in this present time—hymns of today that may be sung together by people who know the thought of the age, and are not afraid that any truth of science will destroy religion, or any revolution on earth overthrow the kingdom of heaven. Therefore this is a hymn of trust and joy and hope.

Truly, Henry Jackson van Dyke did what he said—he penned a hymn of trust and joy and hope, putting them in the right order. When we see God's goodness and love, we trust him. When we trust him, our hearts applaud, and joy abounds. And when joy is rising, hope is as strong as ever and carries us to victory in the midst of strife. What a gift this author has given us in these words! He has offered us a hymn of joy to guide us though our days, teaching us to worship God and applaud his love, and encouraging us toward the triumphal ending of history.

On that day, the stars will begin the song, and we mortals will happily join in, singing, "Joyful, joyful, we adore Thee, God of glory, Lord of love . . ." And the universe, no doubt, will arise in a great standing ovation for God.

∾ *Father God, my heart joins the mighty chorus that endlessly sings your praises. We celebrate your love and grace, we glorify your name, we bow in humble obedience to the Creator of joy. Amen.*

CONCLUSION

Her Name Was Joy

MARY HOLLINGSWORTH

✤

*H*er name was Joy. She was the only real person I'd ever known who was actually named Joy. In her early sixties, she was tall, big-boned, and not so very pretty. But Joy was oh so warm and wonderful. A happy, laughing, delightful lady, she taught our junior high girls' Sunday school class in Farmersville, Texas—a metropolis of 998 nice people and one old grouch.

With twinkling eyes, Joy teasingly said her *real* name was "Josephine Elizabeth Orangeblossom." And when you asked where she lived, she said, "I live on Plumb-and-Nearly Street— it's plumb out of town and nearly in the country."

Joy taught us to memorize important things from the Bible, like all sixty-six books of the Bible, all the prophets, all the kings of Israel and Judah, all the tribes of Israel, the Golden Rule, the

Lord's Prayer, the Beatitudes, the Ten Commandments, and the like. Eventually, we learned them so well that Joy had us recite them in front of our church family. We were so proud! Not to mention our parents, especially my preacher father.

I still remember many of the things Joy taught us. Over the years I have absorbed them as my own. And I never recite one of them today without thinking of sweet Joy.

One of the children's picture books I wrote several years ago is entitled *Christmas in Happy Forest*. And I'm sure it's no surprise that the main character in the book is a teacher named Josephine Elizabeth Orangeblossom, who lives just outside Happy Forest in a tree trunk on Plumb-and-Nearly Street.

And it occurred to me recently that Joy was not only her given name but also her gift of heart and spirit. She lived up to her name in so many ways. And I know that Joy's joy came from the great amount of time she spent with the Great Joygiver and his Book. It came from sharing the meaning of her name with others, like me. It came from *being* joy, not just being *called* Joy.

Her name was Joy. And when she died, a light flickered out in Texas just as a new star appeared in heaven. And sometimes when I'm all alone, I can hear Joy laughing softly, and I know that all is well in heaven and in my world.

~ *Father, thank you for blessing our lives with eternal hope and everlasting joy. Help us to share that joy with everyone we know by telling them about your Son, Jesus. Amen.*

About the Authors

Patsy Clairmont is an acclaimed speaker whose presentations have thrilled audiences in venues ranging from churches to the Pentagon. She is the author of more than a dozen titles, including *God Uses Cracked Pots*. Her book *I Grew Up Little* is her autobiography, a story of hope. Her latest title is *All Cracked Up*.

Mary Graham is president of Women of Faith (WOF), a division of Thomas Nelson, Inc., which hosts America's largest women's conference. Since 1996, nearly two million women have attended Women of Faith conferences in 60 cities. Mary serves as host for the conference and works closely with speakers and musicians. In the WOF offices, she directs 75 employees and supervises all phases of the ministry, including WOF publishing and recording. Prior to joining Women of Faith, Mary was director of international ministries for Insight for Living. She also invested 22 years with Campus Crusade for Christ International. A graduate of California State University in sociology, her work has taken her to every continent, and she has lived in many parts of the U.S.

Barbara Johnson's outreach, Spatula Ministries, and her many best-selling books, including *Humor Me*, *Plant a Geranium in Your Cranium*, and *Living Somewhere Between Estrogen and Death*, have helped millions of hurting people learn to laugh again. Her latest book is *Humor Me, I'm Your Mother*.

Nicole Johnson is a gifted writer and dramatist whose powerful vignettes about life and an ever-faithful God have touched millions of hearts at Women of Faith conferences. The host of *Mid-Point* on the Hallmark channel, Nicole's latest book is *The Invisible Woman*.

Marilyn Meberg has enjoyed a lifetime of careers aimed at helping others: as an instructor at Biola University for ten years, then as a professional therapist, and now as a laughter-loving Women of Faith speaker and author. Her newest book is entitled *Since You Asked*.

Luci Swindoll, world traveler, celebrates life wherever she goes. A former oil company executive and vice president of Insight for Living, she was a pioneer in the contemporary Christian women's book market with titles such as *You Bring the Confetti, God Brings the Joy*. Her latest book is *Life! Celebrate It*.

Sheila Walsh uses words—sung, written, and spoken—to bring hope to millions. Born in Scotland, Sheila became a U.S. citizen in 2003. Her latest releases are *The Best of Sheila Walsh*, a collection of inspirational Celtic music; and *The Heartache No One Sees*.

Thelma Wells is president of A Woman of God Ministries in Dallas and travels globally teaching others to overcome barriers. She holds a master's degree in pastoral ministry and mentors women in the U.S., India, and Africa. Her book *Girl! Have I Got Good News for You* is used as a Christian college curriculum. Her latest title is *Listen Up, Honey*.

OTHER SELECTIONS FOR WOMEN OF FAITH

Best-Selling authors and Women of Faith® speakers Patsy Clairmont, Mary Graham, Barbara Johnson, Marilyn Meberg, Grammy Award Winning singer Sandi Patty, Luci Swindoll, Sheila Walsh, Thelma Wells and dramatist Nicole Johnson bring humor and insight to women's daily lives. Sit back, exhale, and enjoy spending some time with these extraordinary women!

WOMEN OF FAITH®

Contagious JOY 2006

2006 EVENT CITIES & SPECIAL GUESTS

FEBRUARY 23-25
NATIONAL
FT. LAUDERDALE, FL
BankAtlantic Center

MARCH 31-APRIL 1
SHREVEPORT, LA
CenturyTel Center
Avalon, Kathy Troccoli,
Anita Renfroe,
Donna VanLiere

APRIL 7-8
HOUSTON, TX
Toyota Center
Avalon, Max Lucado,
Chonda Pierce,
Donna VanLiere

APRIL 21-22
SPOKANE, WA
Spokane Arena
Avalon, Natalie Grant,
Anita Renfroe

APRIL 28-29
COLUMBUS, OH
Nationwide Arena
Natalie Grant,
Anita Renfroe,
Jennifer Rothschild

JUNE 2-3
OMAHA, NE
Qwest Center
Avalon, Anita Renfroe,
Tammy Trent,
Donna VanLiere

JUNE 9-10
ROCHESTER, NY
Blue Cross Arena
Avalon, Kathy Troccoli,
CeCe Winans,
Donna VanLiere

JUNE 16-17
FRESNO, CA
SaveMart Center*
Avalon, Natalie Grant,
Max Lucado,
Donna VanLiere

JUNE 23-24
ATLANTA, GA
Philips Arena
Avalon,
Nichole Nordeman,
Sherri Shepherd,
Donna VanLiere

JULY 7-8
CHICAGO, IL
United Center
Avalon,
Jennifer Rothschild,
CeCe Winans

JULY 14-15
CLEVELAND, OH
Quicken Loans Arena
Avalon, Natalie Grant,
Sherri Shepherd

JULY 21-22
WASHINGTON, DC
MCI Center
Avalon, Chonda Pierce,
Sherri Shepherd

JULY 28-29
CALGARY, ALBERTA
Pengrowth Saddledome*
Avalon, Carried Away,
Max Lucado,
Donna VanLiere

AUGUST 4-5
ST. LOUIS, MO
Savvis Center
Natalie Grant,
Anita Renfroe,
Sherri Shepherd,
Donna VanLiere

AUGUST 11-12
HARTFORD, CT
Hartford Civic Center
Avalon, Carol Kent,
Jennifer Rothschild

AUGUST 18-19
FT. WAYNE, IN
War Memorial Coliseum
Avalon, Natalie Grant,
Carol Kent

AUGUST 25-26
DALLAS, TX
American Airlines Center
Max Lucado,
Robin McGraw,
Jennifer Rothschild

SEPTEMBER 8-9
ANAHEIM, CA
Arrowhead Pond
Avalon, Robin McGraw,
Anita Renfroe

SEPTEMBER 15-16
PHILADELPHIA, PA
Wachovia Center
Avalon, Robin McGraw,
Nicole C. Mullen

SEPTEMBER 22-23
DENVER, CO
Pepsi Center
Max Lucado,
Chonda Pierce,
Kathy Troccoli

SEPTEMBER 29-30
SACRAMENTO, CA
ARCO Arena
Avalon, Robin McGraw,
Nichole Nordeman

OCTOBER 6-7
OKLAHOMA CITY, OK
Ford Center
Avalon, Max Lucado,
Jennifer Rothschild,
Donna VanLiere

OCTOBER 13-14
PORTLAND, OR
Rose Garden Arena
Avalon, Carol Kent,
Kathy Troccoli,
Donna VanLiere

OCTOBER 20-21
ST. PAUL, MN
Xcel Energy Center
Avalon, Carol Kent,
Anita Renfroe

OCTOBER 27-28
CHARLOTTE, NC
Charlotte Arena
Avalon, Chonda Pierce,
Jennifer Rothschild

NOVEMBER 3-4
VANCOUVER, BC
GM Place*
Avalon, Carried Away,
Nichole Nordeman,
Donna VanLiere

NOVEMBER 10-11
ORLANDO, FL
TD Waterhouse Centre
Avalon,
Nicole C. Mullen,
Anita Renfroe,
Donna VanLiere

NOVEMBER 17-18
PHOENIX, AZ
Glendale Arena*
Avalon,
Nichole Nordeman,
Kathy Troccoli,
Donna VanLiere

1-888-49-FAITH womenoffaith.com

*No Pre-Conference available. Dates, times, locations and special guests subject to change.
Visit womenoffaith.com for details on special guests, registration deadlines and pricing.